T0354291

In the Worst Interest

An Autobiography

JAM

Order this book online at www.trafford.com
or email orders@trafford.com

Most Trafford titles are also available at major online book retailers.

Note for Librarians: A cataloguing record for this book is available from Library
and Archives Canada at www.collectionscanada.ca/amicus/index-e.html

Printed in Victoria, BC, Canada.

ISBN: 978-1-4269-1614-4 (sc)
ISBN: 978-1-4269-1615-1 (dj)

Library of Congress Control Number: 2009935850

*Our mission is to efficiently provide the world's finest, most comprehensive book publishing
service, enabling every author to experience success. To find out how to publish your
book, your way, and have it available worldwide, visit us online at www.trafford.com*

Trafford rev. 1/18/2010

 www.trafford.com

North America & international
toll-free: 1 888 232 4444 (USA & Canada)
phone: 250 383 6864 ♦ fax: 812 355 4082

To my daughters, whom this story is the life we have shared, even if apart.

I pray that together we can write a better final chapter for this life long story.

On any given day in the world a grandfather sits in a rocking chair with his grandchildren sitting on the floor at his feet. He tells them his tale of life. This book is my rocking chair for I may never have my grandchildren ever near me. This is the tale I would tell to them.

On a morning in Montgomery, Alabama Rosa Parks tired from work sat down, simply to rest her feet and for the bus ride home. Racism and indifference held a grip over the United States. The African American fought gallantly in every war from the French Indian to Korean War. Too many people even within our own government, didn't considered them as anything more than non-citizens, didn't belong anywhere but the back of the bus. Just a second class citizen beneath those who thought they were the only ones appropriate for America.

Simply tired of work she sat down and changed the face of our society, racism was about to have its greatest war fought against it. The judge, the jury, the media cast her as a rebel, a misfit. A new voice aroused from that day.

Like Rosa Parks, I too am tired of be made to sit in the back of the bus of emotional abuse, judged as a misfit, a rebel, an outcast to the very society who's constitution I defend and the one I was born into. Still I wait for a new voice to raise again, this voice to reunite divided families and to reaffirm the values of fatherhood.

I offer my thanks to LTC Chairamonte, 1835 Medical Company Combat Stress Control Joint Base Balad, Iraq for encouraging for me to write my story and this life journey. For hope, peace, and love that writing my personal history can bring to all divided families. My prayers and hope for reunion before the final leg of my life journey.

Most importantly I pray this story help future generations with guidance to resolve the serious problems that plague our families, communities and nation. The hope to improve how social service workers and legal representatives relate to all parents regardless good, bad, failures and successful.

For those with the power to judge to take the time to hear all sides of difficult stories and to respond appropriately rather than to judge blindly for power or a lustful will over others of need or have found to be vulnerable.

Note to the reader, this story is a difficult and personal story. It is from my individual perspective and experience with no attempt make up or hide memories for those who know my story. Omissions are unintentional and more of a fading memory that an unwillingness to write.

It is just a story of a life that has seen some of our most difficult issues in society and how a person can grow through experiences endured as a rescuer, a father and as a nurse. The rambling style is that to help push through the emotional trauma as well to give the feel of that grandfather telling his tell to his grandchildren, I know of three that I haven't been able to see.

A story that this writing maybe the only means I will ever get to share the full story to my children and grandchildren.

I have **bold** printed the many quotes I have heard that help made this story. This was mainly to help me recall what was said, when, where, and why.

In the regards of the management of social services, though I hold the profession with high regards, many of the workers I met through this story were unprofessional at best and help create a needless action that blacken the professions eye.

Still I know many workers start with good intentions and some become jade with the difficulties the job can create. I pray that sharing this story help make their profession better and develop techniques to prevent overzealous ideology and focus service to the needs of families and not the power of county social workers and the blindness of our legal system.

None of us, myself included, have the full right answer and

no one is that good of a judge of character to be able to look in everyone's eyes or face and judge correctly.

Hopefully this story can open a few eyes and hearts that count and we all can learn. No more divided families for someone's selfish need of power or callous act of revenge.

In my life I had the privilege, if it can be called that, to see a very complex issue from three different perspectives, most judges, lawyers, social workers and special interest groups and experts rarely have that kind of opportunity.

My hope is since I was never allowed my side of the story when it was needed, that what was endured can be taught to prevent such stories from ever happening again.

And if by some miracle of God, my grandkids will get to know there was a pure heart within me, no one wanted to look for it.

"Parenting cannot be judge by the thickness of the wallet. It has to be by the character and heart of the person." "Revenge is never justice, for vengeance only defeats justice and silence of the facts only denies the truth."

In 1983 fatherhood was declared obsolete by many county social services, no longer needed, and a new form of social bondage created. It is my experience of this decree against fatherhood that I pray may help others that have endured the same miscarriage of justice, and for those who truly needed the beds my daughter's took solely for the purpose of revenge.

To find the ability to tell a tale as well for the many that can't. Knowing that a little boy beaten unconscious for the 9th and last time by his mother. The county took a father away from his daughters and enforcing a thing called Agency Law while a mother's violence would be ignored.

For the power of the county and the wishes of one mother, two daughters are removed from a caring father, for the belief that a mother could do no harm a son was maimed.

For those family members and close friends that were a positive influence during difficult times, I thank you for your love and support. There have been so many others that help make this story. My failure to name you in this book wasn't intentional. This book is built on the idea that through these pages we all can heal.

For the harshness of this story some names are not mentioned.

CHILDHOOD

On a Saturday late in October 1973 the last images of our dad was lying in a hospital bed. He was dying of a massive and aggressive tumor that took him away from our family. Though I was the oldest boy in the family, my sister was two years older; I had become the man of the house at 12 years old.

On a Monday we were pulled from school and took the week to prepare for the funeral and his internment in Sauk City, Wisconsin the place he grew up. He was buried near his father's grave, Grandpa died of the same type of cancer just a few years prior.

One of the last projects that dad had took on was to relocated as many saplings as possible from the silver maple tree in our yard. Our garden had become a tree farm and dad tried to give as many of the saplings a chance to grow rather than to weed the garden that was always planted each year.

Some of the trees would be planted in the grade school yard were us kids went to school. He had removed the poison ivy that filled the little woods behind the school and a nature trail was laid. He had a strong bond to the natural world. 32 saplings would be planted in the ½ lot that was part of our yard. On the day of his passing I took consol by clenching a maple leaf, from one of those trees, one of the last things my dad and I shared.

The fall colors were at their peak on the drive from the twin city area to small farm town in south central Wisconsin. The wake in South Saint Paul, Minnesota in the days prior to the funeral had many dignitaries from both the state and federal government offices. Our dad was a simple machinist who on his spare time was a lobbyist for the American Hoist and Derrick Machinist Union.

Not a well paid professional lobbyist, but an everyday Joe lobbyist, he gave people a voice. His tours of the state capital served me better than anything to expect and was handy for the future events of my life.

Dad, I do miss you so.

THE BEGINNINGS OF A JOURNEY

Minnesota late 1970's

The late evening calm is punctured by the banshee shrill of tones and beeps, the dispatcher declares "Fire Rescue, Unknown Rescue at..." For me it was a 300 meter sprint to the fire station, many times I would man the call desk, recording the call's information, mainly because I was under age. I could let another adult take the truck. But this is how my story began, responding to calls for help.

Us kids on the youth program trained with the adults. Learned the procedures and tactics of the fire fighter, to man the radio desk, cleaned the station while the trucks were gone and the equipment when the trucks came back. Sometimes the gear they used was covered in blood, in the days prior to HIV even the body's bags were cleaned after they returned from the coroner's office with hot soapy bleach water.

On their return to the station the pain on the guys faces were noted, a person was badly abused, beaten, or injured and unknown if the person would survive. Another time that almost seems like another world with a lifetime in between. Sometimes I feel I have lived multiple lifetimes in just one life.

JAM

In the late 1970's child abuse and domestic violence was still a behind closed doors issue; it wouldn't be until 1983 that a big change in county social services would occur. This change would have a huge impact in my life. Not an enjoyable or as memorable change as anyone would ever like or even be beneficial as many hoped.

In regards to domestic violence two situations that I recall occur not in my community but in nearby suburbs. One situation occurred when a husband became so violently angry at his wife that he beat her with the only thing that was available, an aluminum baseball bat.

One of the responding police officers was my search and rescue explorer post leader.

His description of the scene was horrifying. The husband beat his wife so relentlessly that once the first squad arriving to the scene the police officer discovered her remains dripping from the ceiling and all over the room.

Not all deadly weapons are a gun.

The next incident actually occurs in two parts.

On a weekend the community across the river woke to a murder. A young lady was killed and the houses surrounding the victim's home were sprayed painted with the message, "Your Next".

Turned out the killer was a young high school senior who killed her rival. She claimed to be the next Mary and the boy who had just dumped her for the victim was to become the next Joseph. Too mentally ill to be tried she went into the mental health system. After about six months she had her first weekend on her own and disappeared.

Her remains would be found months later in the Mississippi River next to a bridge in our community. She had jumped off a bridge in St. Paul and drowned in the middle of January, we recovered her remains in April.

Next lesson learn: women also can kill.

My high school days spent first as a youth member on the local volunteer fire department, then a short period as an

4

Emergency Medical Technician and probationary fire fighter prior to entering active duty army as a medic.

Still the days between spring of 1976 and the morning I climbed into the army recruiters sedan in June 1980 was one part of this journey. Over 600 times I would stop whatever it was that I was doing, and for not even a dime gave up some time to help someone in need, regardless of why.

Some of the calls had lifelong effects to all involved. Critical Incident Debriefing had not been developed yet and **"Post Traumatic Stress could only happen to war vets, not anyone else."** This was the accepted mentality even at that it was more a stigma than a mental or emotional health issue, a reason to reject a cause for suffrage.

My first serious car accident a friend of my sister was killed when this young lady ,angry at her boy friend sped off in the car on a residential street, going too fast the car slid against a curb and was sent rolling across a lawn stopping on the roof and against the house. She was trapped between the top of the seat and the roof, never recovering from her wounds and died by the following morning.

There were many such accidents; the majority occurred in a deadly intersection that was finally replaced with an overpass.

One weekend a classmate of mine house caught fire and her little brother died in the fire. Facing the pain in her face when she came back to school was a lot to bear, I had much to learn.

One thing I learn was to talk about the trauma, rather than holding it in. Decades before mental health services would encourage anyone who faces the trauma to talk about it; up to now talking about it was a sign of weakness.

The other pain I faced was that of the mild mannered fire fighter who had fell through what was the basement door and landing on the child's remains, the stairs had already been burned away. He was a father himself. One of his kids would graduate from high school with me, but his kids and I never hung out with each other we were involved with two very different crowds.

There were also many grassfires that we kids responded too. Grassfire response in a suburban area is very labor intensive; the youth program was often pressed into service so that enough personnel can be sent to the scene. With three railroads right of ways through our city spring and fall had more than enough grassfires to contend with.

During one Sunday morning grassfire call we responded to a plane crash. A small plane took off from a nearby small airport and had ran out of fuel right after takeoff, I had just sent a water truck to the grass fire to refill the trucks, but the driver got to witness the plane as it bounced off the roof of a house. So with church in full swing I sounded the siren on the hill to get everyone to the station, keyed the tones and the telephone. It has the most manic ten minutes of my life, but I was doing something very purposeful and with deep meaning and self reward.

One of the most serious accidents happened on a November night in 1979 we would respond to a car accident were a 19 year old young man would be burned alive. We responded as fast as we could, to the station, the scene. His life was over before the first fire truck could reach him.

My seat at the radio desk heard his final screams as the police updated the status and location. He was a popular kid in the community, most of the fire fighters on that first truck had graduated from high school with him the past summer, and I would be doing the same with his sister for the following spring. Still his scream remain embedded for life, I could no longer taken in a horror flick with too much screaming.

The next day at school graffiti was etched in my wall locker declaring me a murder since many classmates felt we didn't respond fast enough to the call. The first truck had arrived on the scene in less than 4 minutes, considering it was suppertime when the tones went off and no one was in the station.

Monday nights we trained between, first aid and fire fighter skills, and reviewed the past weeks runs. What calls I can remember from those days become only a small handful, car accidents, fires, child abuse, a woman beaten by her husband, a heart attack where a toddler child would ask me if her daddy would die, a drug addict with a gun now mostly vague memories of my high school years.

During our training nights a few mishaps occurred Gary, in charge of one live fire drill tried to get the fire going by tossing a coffee can of diesel/gas mix into the structure as, unknown to him, four of us were inside mainly just crawling around when our world lit up. How all of us escaped without injury, even today I would have to claim hand of God. Sadly in three weeks after our incident another fire department in Colorado would have a deadly accident with live fire training and federal rules would be put in place.

I still remember the feeling being in the room were the explosion occurred, the feel of the air pressure as the fuel mix ignited, though I was crawling on the floor when the flash of the flames shot between my legs.

I started to pray as I dropped completely to the floor and started flowing water to cool the air around me so I could make my escape. The best estimate was that we were in the building for a total less than 3 minutes; still it caused damage to my gear. I was still wearing the old fashion rubber fire coats of that time were just being phased out by Nomex.

At my first live fire training we were burning an old farm house. Us boys found a jar of white liquid and threw into the fire; it stunk as it burned in the fire. The lesson would never be forgotten. Later in the drill m fire captain and I made an entry, this was my first time in a burning building. We crawled past the burning bales of hay and wood debris the windows were boarded up with plywood so to help keep the building dark.

Up the stairs we went to practice search and rescue techniques, but I bumped the trim of the door upstairs door as we cleared the stairs and the air mask was pulled from my face, I was inhaling at that same moment and all I got was a lung full of smoke. I let myself slide down the stairs and out the door when trying to clear the smoke from my mask failed. Unlike the modern air masks used today the old system was like scuba gear, you had to draw a breath to get the diaphragm open and air to be released from the bottle on my back. It was that action that got so much smoke in my lungs when the mask lifted off my face, outside I coughed and gagged for nearly 45 minutes. Since then on I would never take up smoking.

When the structures became too unsafe to train in we would completely burn the remains to keep curious out of the ruins and getting hurt. At another live burn house it had rained much of the afternoon and the ruins wouldn't light, we found a stash of old tires in the yard and handed them off into the foundation. We forgot the remove the valves from the tires that were still on rims. Once the fire got hot enough the tires ruptured. Another fire fighter and I were walking past that side when it happened, his eyebrows were burnt off and we were just missed by a piece of wood that flew past us. We had walked around to make sure that nothing else was burning outside of the house foundation.

My mom didn't take the fire department idea well; at first she was reluctant fearing that it may turn me into a heavy drinker. Beer was sold in a soda machine in the kitchen right in the station. Still the expectations were high, we weren't allowed to buy or consume beer at the fire station.

We had to maintain a better than "C" average grades in school. We were not allowed to skip school for fire calls, **"If the fire is that big the fire department would come and get us if needed, otherwise if it is that large we can help after school."**

All I needed to do was look and see if there is smoke or hear the siren sound to know I would need to take the bus home, because I was heading for the fire station instead.

Once I came of age to be accepted on the department as a probationary fire fighter I started riding the trucks rather than sitting behind the desk. Now I got to fully experience what I once only listen too over the air waves. I lived close enough to make the first truck out the door.

The week before Christmas 1979 I was finally given permission to ride the trucks as a probationary fire fighter.

That week started out dry, on the evening of the 21st the fire department was called to an abandoned campfire in a small city park. The afternoon of the 22nd wet met with a heavy wet snow and dropping air temperatures that froze the snow to the street surface. As soon as rush hour started so did the car accidents.

There were accidents everywhere and it was nonstop. There was no supper for me that night. As soon as we returned from one accident another accident call was dispatched. It seemed like if it was a major intersection in the city there was an accident there at some point of the night. An older gentleman in one housing section developed a heart attack shoveling snow.

Once back from the chest pain medical I finally was able to return all the way home. Supper was cold and in the refrigerator. As I had some cold supper and readied for bed my scanner picked up a call for a neighboring fire department to a car accident that was just north of our cities border. The city police was alerted for an unknown medical to the same address.

Supper was dropped and back to the fire station I went.

At the fire station several fire fighters had been hanging around conversing, unaware that another emergency was occurring in the city. They never heard the radio call for the police nor noticed the address the neighboring department was responding to.

They thought I was kidding about the call, but the telephone went into its steady unending ring signaling an emergency call had been received, radio tones followed. Everyone headed to their lockers and geared up for the call.

Like the police it was reported as an unknown medical, the same address as the neighboring fire department was responding to. It would take them at least three more minutes before arriving and we will have nearly a 10 minute response to the address it was a remote intersection in the city and beyond the reach of either department.

The rescue squad was still on the road when the first truck

reported and verified as a single vehicle accident with five seriously injured passengers. The second rescue squad on our department as well as both pumpers went en route, requested for all the help that would be needed.

By the time my truck arrived to the scene there was 4 police cars, two sheriff cars and a Minnesota Highway Patrol on the scene along with three rescue squads, two pumpers, a grass truck, two ambulances and a tow truck.

The injuries of the patients would basically clean out all the supplies the rescue squads carried, with one of the rescue squads transporting one of the patients to the hospital.

In the car was a Boy Scouting friend of mine. He was out partying with his older friends and all were very drunk. Traveling at a high rate of speed the driver drove through the wrong side of a "T" intersection, launched in the air caused by a higher hill to the house side of the ditch and flew over a 30' pine tree. The under carriage parts were left hanging randomly in the tree looking like it had been done purposely as an original holiday decoration. Everyone survived, most with lifelong disabilities my scouting friend was never the same.

Christmas Day a friend of mine would lose his home to a fire. His family holiday tradition was to go to all the relatives before opening the presents at home. So on this fateful day the presents at home were still under the tree as the house caught fire.

This was an old house that had a fuel oil furnace, propane kitchen stove and a wood burner stove as well. It was the wood burner that caused the fire. My first job was to protect the propane tank that the fire was now only inches to. It was sad to see the presents and the kids' toys and collectables that were destroyed in the fire and also to find the remains of the family dog in the middle of the living room.

In February 1980 we had a structure fire in a middle of a blizzard, -20 and high winds made for a very uncomfortable job. I got to the station just in time to be the crew on the water truck. Since the address did not have a hydrant nearby there was the need to shuttle water from a mile and a half away to the fire. Since it was so cold no one rode on the back of the trucks to and from the scene. The attempt was to protect us from as much as possible from the cold.

For me it was set up the hydrant, fill the tank and as the two water trucks shuttled together delivering water to the scene. Each time we got out of the truck we would get wetter and wetter from all the moving water. Soon the trips would be too short to warm the chilled and wet body from the cold outside. On the last trip we actually entered the smoldering building to warm back up.

Some of the calls had violent themes, a drug over dose call just doors away from my house had the neighbor pulling a gun on me as my mom, who had ran out the door behind me, screaming that he had a gun, as he pulled it from his jacket.

I had never seen so many police cars ever show up at one time. I had fled the scene and was safely at my yard when the first squad pulled up. My mom told the police officer what had happen and the police took it from there. I now know what it felt like to have life threaten by deadly force. It wasn't the best feeling to ever have, fear never felt so lonely.

A grassfire in the May of 1980 had both my brother and I working different parts of the line. The fire department had changed the youth program that I grew up with into an award winning Fire Service Boy Scouts Explorer Post which my brother joined. This school day fire started at 10 am. By the time we got out of school the fire was still burning.

The fire had been started by a freight train and crossed nearly the entire county. Every available fire department and fire fighter worked the line. We would not get home until 2 am and we still had school in the morning. During the fire my brother gained a burn to the tip of his nose.

Still those memories shaped my personality as well as what I looked forward to in life. By the time I left the fire department I had counted over 500 responses with the youth program and nearly 100 responses as a probationary fire fighter in four years.

I was looking ahead, four years in the army. Come back and go to paramedic school with the educational benefits at least that was the plan, but then again people and circumstances change. With those changes so does the direction of life.

The final week of school I was approached by one of the bullies from the 11th grade. He was cursing me for being on the fire department, and taunting my decision to join the military. That night I would be at the scene of a fatal car accident that he and his buddy were killed. The next day at school I was tired for being up all night and all the other students wanted to talk about some accident, it wasn't tell lunch did I realize they were talking about the same accident I was at.

The weekend before basic training would have me running to the fire station, we all look at each other in disbelief. "Did she say, fishing spear in foot?" there were 5 us that climb on board of our light rescue squad as we headed down the street to the address.

The sun had just started the day as we tried to mentally picture what we were to see once we arrived, it was nothing we ever could had ever pictured. Even with the address in a trailer park gave the setting of a bad joke brewing.

A 12 year old boy was stabbed in the foot by his little brother with dad's frogging spear; the junior of the two was losing in an early morning game of lawn darts, waking up dad in the commotion.

Luckily his aim was as bad with the spear as with the lawn darts, the big toe was nicked, but the tennis shoe, sock, and spear were destroyed trying to work through the situation, all with foot firmly anchored to the ground.

That call was the morning of June 6th 1980. Most of my day was spent getting the house ready for my graduation party on Saturday. My brothers and I gave up our rooms in the house for our relatives from Wisconsin; we would slumber in a tent in the yard. However sleep would come late for us since we spent the evening at our neighbor's celebrating their daughter's birthday and we would not hit the bed until 1 am. Lighting could be seen in the distance.

We barely got our eyes shut when mom came outside and had us seek shelter in the house; we dropped the tent and secured it to the ground so it wouldn't be blown apart. The storm hit with a fury and the lighting was close together and the thunder was deafening, as soon as the power went out the fire department monitor began its banshee shrill.

It was almost 2am when the first storm related call came in the lighting interfered with the radio transmission all you could hear was static. We left the comfort of the house and headed into the storm. The wind was so strong running to the station was impossible, and the rain was in heavy sheets. The best we could do was a struggled walk against the wind to the station.

This time my brother took the radio I grabbed my gear and climbed into the fire chief's sedan, by now every truck had been sent out into the storm each to a different address and other address were stacking up waiting for someone to become available to respond. All we could do was respond to one scene, wait for the power company then respond to another.

All the police officers were recalled to help respond to all the different scenes as well as public works employees. By 3am the entire staff of the city was out of bed and in the storm. The crew I was with stood by a downed power line on one street near the address of that bitter winter night call and would wait nearly an hour before a power company truck arrived and relieved us.

As we left that scene we were stopped by a motorcyclist who was riding in the storm, reporting that a power line across another road broke as he was riding past, he was shaking heavily from the near miss of the high tension line, we went en route to the scene.

The storm was still going strong and by now we had debris falling from the sky. As we crest the hill we saw the wires dancing on the pavement, sparks flying everywhere, we were going too fast to stop and ran over the power lines. Sparks lit up the car interior. We met up with a police officer from a neighboring community on the other side of the downed power lines, spoke briefly then drove back around the scene.

What should have taken less than 5 minutes would take nearly a half hour. We would pull up short distances to clear the street of debris before going another short distance and do it all over again. Once at the needed intersection we took our stand to close off the street and watch the sunrise as the storm finally abated.

A Minnesota Highway Patrolman stopped by to assess which road was feasible for trucks to use to move the freight they were carrying. However the storm had a massive path and he told dispatch to hold the trucks at the Wisconsin boarder, no trucks would be moving anytime soon all major roads were closed due to the mess that the storm left behind. The power company arrived and the highway patrolman relieved us from the scene.

As we returned to our station we found that no one escaped the wrath of this storm, the station flag pole was bent like a paperclip. My brother said as he sat the desk he watched it begin to spin and then it bent like a hand had been taken to it and the guys that were at the station had to work together to bend it out of the street. It was morning and we hadn't had any sleep yet, so we returned home.

Sleep was only a short nap when the next round of calls came in. So the day of my graduation party was filled with brief moments of calm, maybe a short nap, then periods of house to house as the power company would get one set of down power lines fix, turn the power back on briefly to find even more breaks in the system. This would last the entire weekend.

My graduation party consisted of mostly the kids from the fire department youth program, family and one of the police officers stopped by. As the party started the banshee cry of tones would sound once again for a motorcyclist who had left the road and wrapped himself in a barbed wire fence near the high school. This time a mob would do the run from my house and to the fire station.

Another fire fighter gave me a ride in his car to the station, cutting across the ditch that separated the street in front of my house. The soft dirt nearly got the car stuck and the tire marks remained for years beyond.

By Monday I had only managed about four hours of sleep for the entire weekend, and this day was full of meetings and farewells from the fire department and the city leadership and the promise from the fire department that I would have my position held, on the fire department leadership's request I put in for military leave.

Tuesday morning came with the army recruiter arriving at my door shortly after returning from my last trip to the fire station. Some sleep would be had on the flight, but mainly the big change in my life made sleep difficult at best.

Bedtime at Ft. Lenard Wood, Missouri would come until after midnight and in the dark hours of Wednesday morning. Out like a rock, only to be awaken by the lights being turned on and someone yelling **"On, you're Feet!"** In mid air I realized I had taken the top bunk and bounced off the bed next to mine. I was in the army now.

By the time I would get up that morning I would have less than 10 hours of sleep in 5 days, punchy would have been an understatement and sleep deprived wouldn't even come close to the description, but my group would have a weekend delay before going to our basic training companies, already I was homesick from the fire trucks. But the bed for now beckons. I slept the weekend away.

Emergency Services had gotten into my blood, not as a phase but as a life style I would identify who I was in my life, the world and for God. An idea of simple service to the community was my greatest gift, with personal drive and sense of belonging.

As a senior in high school I took the Emergency Medical

Technicians course at Inver Hills Community College. Since I gave up study hall time to work in the school offices my guidance counselor and school principle got to see my progress. Up to now only gifted student could become involved with the advance placement program. My college transcript helped the school district set up an agreement with the college. The new policy would allow any student taking a college class have those credits added to their high school diploma.

My 4 credits unfortunately would not be able to get on my high school transcript; the policy for me was too late, but a new door had been opened for others to follow. By the time I left the active duty army that policy would be a nationwide educational policy for many high school students.

An additional involvement with the Municipal Affairs Commission, my high school days were fully beyond school dance and parties, I had grown up quick and not as a part of a large group, just small tight knit teams with a higher purpose and beyond one's self and focused on the community needs.

We helped get a new city hall through the voters, a stop sign on a dangerous intersection and an exotic pet ordinance, which would later become the foundation of a Minnesota State Statute, forbidding all exotic pets from the metro area.

One of the commission members was a nurse who worked in a local hospital emergency room. In the spring of 1980 I got invited to spend the night in her ER since I was a registered Emergency Medical Technician. It was an experience of a lifetime and added in my preparation to the time I would spend on active duty. During that night a drunk would assault one of the doctors and I broke the fight up while the doctor ran to get security.

Looking back I could see the periods that the first thing I did would pray, the training accident, a badly injured woman who was hit by a drunk driver, the car that jumped the pine tree, the prayer wasn't loud just to myself for guidance, for strength, for courage.

There were times when the situation was so violent and

fast, the reaction was like auto-pilot, never fully understanding neither the situation or my reaction to it, yet a prayer brought solace and peace to what had just happen as well as finding the right course of action.

The fire department had become such a big part of me, it was my father figure. Since my dad had died of a massive brain tumor a few years before I joined, and I got to know the guys who responded that October morning very well they stood in place that my dad's death vacated.

One last thing I would take with me from high school was a quote by a math teacher over computers; **"Unless you are in math or science honors you will never see a computer in your lifetime."** Like the automobile and telephone a passing fad that would never reach the average citizens of the world.

But, it was now a new day, and new ways. The army really started shaping my distrust of peer pressure; my high school days on the fire department left me an outsider to many of my classmates. Only the fellow students on the fire department or scouting did I have much contact with. At times it seemed that the army just made that divide between peers and me even wider.

Still there was basic at Fort Leonard Wood, Missouri and two schools at Ft Sam Houston, Texas before I got my assignment at Reynolds Army Community Hospital, Ft. Sill, Oklahoma.

At Ft Sam I would meet two young ladies that would have an effect on my developing dating and interrelationship skills.

First there was Dianne. She was from Michigan and had just dropped out of dental technician school. I first met her at the club on post and the following weekend spent it together. This was my first real attempt at a sexual relationship, which was pretty much over as the weekend ended.

The following two weekends she wouldn't even give me eye contact. About three weeks later, she was at the bar when she starting to show signs of a stroke. I went with her to the hospital to help comfort her and help her get the care she needed. Afterwards we wrote back and forth for a short while, it finally drifted away.

In her last letter she claimed I had gotten her pregnant, but not to worry, she had already found someone else in her life and we parted. She would have been between the fourth and fifth month if that was true and at that first time she told me she was pregnant and she had already moved on.

Then there was Sue, of Philipino descent she took my heart, but as with many first, her interest changed, even though the friendship stayed. My wooing her failed, the most serious letters lasts for over a year, she gave me something to look forward to each time I opened my mail box.

While still at Fort Sam Houston Sue broke her ankle on evening. I had literally gotten into a heated argument with the charge of quarters for an ambulance, then first aid supplies. Both where refused, but a broken down pick-up truck was called and we were taken to the hospital.

After carrying her to the emergency room a nurse looking over her injury stated, **"Oh my God, I should had sent the ambulance for you."** Turned out both the nursing staff and the CQ got into some hot water in how that situation was handled.

I continued on with my training. As for Sue, she became a training holdover and was sent to Ft. Bragg after her ankle healed after she was allowed to complete her training.

Still we wrote often and a confident relationship had grown. In the days before calling cards, I had third party called her through mom. Hard thing was I never knew how much I owed mom for the calls. Funny thing was our relationship hadn't become sexual, but it has remained a very strong lasting and friendship that still exist today.

In between the first and second course that I was taking our group had a two week hold. During this time we were assigned different details that kept us busy. I was never a person to get hung up on small details, I would always find away to get the job done with some enjoyment rather than get bent out of shape over. This positive attitude even when doing some difficult or demeaning work worked for me. I was often released from duties early rather than have addition dumped on me once I got the job done.

The first week I started helping at the Academy of Health Sciences Building working in a small supply room and selling tickets for some officer gathering. Tuesday we painted a recreation hall. Wednesday was helping at the base laundry. Though all the laundry got done the group had a lot of fun, between the sheets, pillow cases and blankets. Thursdays I had an accident with the riding lawn mower against an old pole anchor that was hidden in the long grass.

Friday came at everyone was sent to their assigned details and I was left standing, alone. The sergeant came up to me as everyone had left; **"First Sergeant says you're having too much fun on the details. You are to vanish for the day and don't be seen. Be here at closing formation and we don't think you'll get into trouble, however if you do there will be hell to pay. You're dismissed."** They same thing happened for the second week. I showed up for formation than vanished for the day only on the final Friday of that two week period the whole group got the extra time off.

It is ironic to think, my grandfather in World War One had volunteer for extra opportunities to work as a KP so he could get extra food rations. He had been a handful for sergeants and medics alike in his brief time as a heavy artilleryman in the Wisconsin National Guard. Here I was getting kick off details and sent out on my own. I toured the base and its multiple museums.

Once the second course was done at Fort Sam everyone was sent to their on the job training sites and from there our final assignments. I was assigned to Reynolds Army Community Hospital Fort Sill, Oklahoma. I would be assigned to the emergency room and ambulance section. I was assigned there by the hospital commander himself. It was a great fit and was back working emergencies again.

The biggest burden would occur when Sue was raped by an army reserve officer who was on his units' annual training (AT). He got off simply because the army let him go home since the rape occurred late in his AT period and policy at that time didn't recall personnel to active duty for criminal investigations and misconduct, Sue had been betrayed by the army. Sue was deeply hurt, I had immediately spent the weekend with her, but the trauma was too great for her and by her request we made our separate ways, back at Ft. Sill to recover from such a roller coaster ride of emotions.

Once back there were some harsh situations that I faced, one week we had a young soldier come in, and he had been gang raped by his squad leader and the squad leader's wife. As we prep the victim for the rape exam the on call social worker arrived to the E.R.

The next thing that happened was sickening. The social worker took such objection to the idea of this kid to make such a claim; he was more worried about some female that had to be raped by this villain, since **"No man could ever be a rape victim."**

The social worker never entered the room, just degraded the poor kid in the hallway and he eventually threw a rape kit into the room and at the doctor. Our doctor was so mad that the social worker was forced out of the E.R. on the spot. I don't know who was more confused or mad the patient or the medical staff at what had happened. Still for this male victim even the MP's had a difficult time trying to get the case together since the victim was male and no one was prepared to handle such a situation.

The following weekend I would have two near rape encounters against me. The first was a total stranger that I was able to talk my way out, the other a Staff Sergeant friend and co-worker that I had to fight my way out. We went up to Oklahoma City for the day just to get off Fort Sill. On the way back he began to act strange and I was getting uncomfortable. He wouldn't keep his hands to himself and I was finding the need to sit closer to the passenger door constantly pushing his hand off me.

I had put my bicycle in his room before the trip and went to get it when he began to force himself on me. Trying to wrestle me down and remove my pants. At one point I was able to throw him against the wall cracking the wall through both sides. Still if the army couldn't take the story of the young GI, who sat bleeding in our exam room earlier in the week, how was I to report what had just happened?

The only real grace was the severe damage to the wall that would not be explained. 1SG figured something very wrong had happen; the sergeant took a transfer to a west coast military entrance processing station and was never seen again. Still no one to talk too and no report taken, and no penetration meant no crime had occurred. No other services were available for men **"Rapes never happen to men."**

I often wonder how the near miss with rape threat had affected me. This is one of the reasons I struggle in relating to other people, or have such a hard time making friends?

Was this the reason I struggled with my own personal level of anger? Is this were some of the darkest foundations of PTSD within me?

MEETING MY FIRST WIFE

By now the hospital got a new chaplain assistant, and we started making some connection. It was far from a perfect match; still she was someone to relate with, to talk to.

Since much of my attempts at dating fell flat, I found myself with some success with her and was enjoying the company. However, something wasn't quite right and a little over two month I called off dating to collect my thoughts.

About three months later I started fancying the idea of volunteering for a tour to Alaska, I had told her of the idea and she suggested we try dating again.

This time in period of less than two months we bought a car together and rented an apartment, and started a sexual relationship. Within three months she would become pregnant and I was overjoyed, I was going to be a father.

Starting to look forward to fatherhood, we started discussing her taking a maternity discharge so she could focus on raising a child, my pay alone with housing and substance allowance would be close, but do able.

The plan was to save money, get married and have a baby, but first she wanted to cut some costs as we prepared, wanting to stay with my mother while we planned the wedding.

She rejected any idea of going back to her home state of California, **"Too many blacks and wetbacks"** she would always claim. Besides there were too many problems with her family to raise a child in, she was never going back to California.

About Christmas time 1981 we moved her into my old bedroom back home. I would send most of my meager check home to help her and return to living in the barracks.

The next six months was a drawn out long distance relationship, still anxiously waiting for my first born, proud to soon to become a father and a husband. I started to become blind to small problems that were beginning to show.

During the winter of 1982 domestic violence and child abuse would visit the ER on a regular basis.

A couple harsh nights come to mind. A policy had been coming through the social services which simply stated; protect the woman at all costs. A domestic in the southern most housing area on base tested that theory.

The theory was only men could be abusive, their usually bigger, stronger, so we had to enjoy being abusive. A woman on the other hand could only be a victim, never causing a thought of abuse unless forced to do so.

So then there was this night, waiting a block away, to be cleared in by the MP's. We watch as the dad was chased out of the house as mom is hitting him with a cast iron pan. The MP's tried to approach the scene as he was struck square in the face, we heard the bones of his face break were we where parked.

Yet, it was the brand new policy endorsed and created by Women Advocates that had to be followed, under threat of law suits it was taught, mom regardless of any visible injury was to be taken to the hospital first.

The father with his injuries had to be according to the policy, handcuff and detained. He would not be allowed any healthcare, unit the doctor had seen the mom and was allowed to record "her" injuries and the police report secured.

The problem was dad's injuries were beginning to threaten

his very life and the ambulance was dispatched to the MP Station to pick him up, his condition wouldn't wait for policy.

Still social services declared the "War of the Roses" and the social worker demanded our reports reflect the **"Proper Theory"** of domestic violence regardless of the facts of the case, or what we witnessed.

None of us, between the ambulance run report, or the MP incident report was changed, both parents would be charged with mutually fighting. The rift between law enforcement and social worker would start develop.

Prior to sending my girlfriend to stay with my mother there was the neighbor whose wife stabbed her husband in the chest with an ice pick during a heated argument.

We loaded him into the ambulance and he was rushed to the hospital, his heart had been punctured. Time was running out fast. I no longer remember if he lived or not. It was days before the move, it wouldn't be the only time I would experience someone with a penetrating wound to the heart.

Still media was pushing women to attack their men and claim him as a threat to her. The county social services would help protect her in claiming him as so abusive that her actions were justifiable. Movies like the **"Burning Bed"** help galvanize the ideology.

TWO KIDS THEN WERE KILLED.

A child was burned to death by the stepfather; a two year old can't handle burns like an adult. This child's pads on his feet cooked on a floor heater grate, burns to both legs to his knees with signs this was done on several occasions for burns were to healing burns. This was the stepfather's idea of potty training.

Shock finally overcame the toddler and he died in the place that was supposed to be home. Stepdad's efforts to resisutate the child involved beating the lifeless remains against a porch pillar, nothing could be done. The army ambulance responded to the scene and bought the child's lifeless body to the E.R.

Shortly afterwards the local ambulance service would bring another child to our ER. Though alive, he was in decompensating shock, his body unable to sustain life with injuries he had. He was only 9 months old. Mom and dad had no story for why the boy was so badly injured, they didn't even showed concern, as we fought to keep him alive, they were laughing and telling jokes to each other.

Dad was only 17, mom had just turned 15. It was the sad combination. A young man dropped out of school, gets a GED, either trouble with the law or convinces his parents to let him join the army.

He became a field artilleryman and shortly after basic sent to South Korea. There he started dating a local girl, who was even younger. They married and had a kid, before they even had a chance to truly become adults. His tour overseas done, he brought his family back to Oklahoma.

Turned out mom and dad both went into a violent rage, because the baby wouldn't stop crying. Now days after the beating he laid with a sickly whimper, slowly dying right in front of us.

The plan was to MEDEVAC the child to a neonatal center in OKC, but the boy died due to his injuries as the Huey's skids touched the land pad there.

It turned out in both cases neighbors repeatedly called for these two boys, the county social services never took a foot out of their offices to intervene or investigate. Military social services did not have the authority to investigate off base issues even if it involved military personnel.

Instead, we were told by our hospital social worker that a national course of action was being developed and if the public got wind of what the policy was going to do, there would be hard time ahead for the family. Social Services had declared war against the family, actually it was fatherhood instead.

During one case of child abuse that was brought to our ER a social made the statement; **"What we** (sic. Social services) **are about to do, will cause a civil war within our nation."**

OUR WEDDING DAY

In the middle of June 1982 my girlfriend packed up and left Minnesota in a hurry. From my mom and youngest brothers pleaded to me to just let her go, something bad had happened. She had become violent and had attacked David my youngest brother.

Within hours my girlfriend calls, begging for forgiveness. Later I found out she had assaulted David very brutally with a broom. Either it was my concerned for the daughter her womb or simply the delay in finding the words to describe what had happen back in Minnesota, it was after the wedding when the story would sink into the brain cells.

My girlfriend had posed a dilemma; if we were going to get married it had to happen now. Otherwise, she would continue back to LA and she would send the baby into adoption never to ever be seen by my eyes ever.

Was I being foolish or stupid or both? For all I had been looking forward to was oldest daughter's birth. For the past 8 and half months I prepared and was so excited, giddy for the day she would be born.

The pain of losing this child of mine was too much for me to bear. My soon to be wife found the way to control me. So from here on she hung to this idea, that if ever I displeased her, she would take it all away, the marriage, the girls, just to destroy me, just to show me how much her anger was going to cost me.

Repeatedly, she would yell at me of each disagreement, how she can deny my rights to the girls, just for making her mad at me. Every argument, over the bills, the car, any disagreement the threat was made, over and over again and again to the point I could never tell why we had the argument in the first place. I just remember the constant threat of never being my children's father, if I angered her enough I would be denied the right to be my child's father.

Still there were peaceful and loving moments as well. It is sad how the most traumatizing memories remain through the years. Camping trips to the Wichita Mountain Wildlife Refuge, and drives into the country side all seem to have disappeared from memory.

After our first daughter was born I could focus on this precious bundle of joy. Many sleepless nights shared with her. I would put her in the chest carrier and take her for a short walk until she fell back to sleep, this is the one moment I cherish the most. Marianne could sleep, we two could get tried enough to sleep and for a moment it was just peace and love, father and daughter time.

During this same time period the media push was to denounce domestic violence as an act of crime of man against woman. **"Only a man processes the will, want and the enjoyment to be violent."**

Actions were being taken to protect women from harsh sentences if they had killed their husbands, assurance by our own media services would declare how the woman actions are driven by the actions an abusive man. Meanwhile men were being completely denounced. Our arguments with our wives were now, **"A sign of a male's willingness to act violently against women."**

Still how does that explain, the child needing clothes, or

the car needing insurance and being degraded for not making enough money for a family, by the person who stood at the altar and said "I do" with you?

The message became clear, whatever a woman would claim, it shall be believe without any means of proof, no need for hard evidence, **"Everyone knows the story anyways why bother with a full investigation"**?

A man on the other hand, even with hard evidence would be question what his motive were because the belief was firmly **"Men are the abusers, and if the man is the one making the allegations then what is he hiding?"** Nothing else needed to be said. Granted there were cases were the guy got lucky. The evidence was so overwhelming that it couldn't be denied could not be hidden from view.

At this same time in Jordan, Minnesota an infamous and complex child abuse case. The effects of that case were felt even in Oklahoma. Regardless of that cases outcome at the time I had no idea how that case would affect my future.

Within months of our first daughter was born my wife would become pregnant with our second. I am glad still in fact of seeing how this life played out that the two sisters could be there for each other, yet others declared me selfish for not letting my wife to simply give the girls up for adoption when she wanted to.

Still I have always had love for my children first, but a new message was being quietly expanding across social services, as spoken by an army reserve counterpart **"If the father can't afford the child, then he must give up the child. Since only thing dads are to do is to pay for their children."**

It had been said in one courtroom **"Though it is compelling that a father loves his children. The only view that the courts cares about is can he pays for his children."** If not then we fathers are a waste to our children's life.

The full effects of REGANOMICS would be felt on this family in over a year after our second daughters' birth. First the army was going to send me to Germany.

JAM

My wife was two months pregnant when I was sent to Germany in March 1983. With the turmoil now in both families our decision was to stay at Ft. Sill, while I completed my tour overseas. Since I refused to extend for the full 3 years and bring my family over with me, it was to be 14 months tour in duration, in which we would return to Minnesota.

Back in Minnesota the promises were still good for my return to the fire department and the career development it would had brought with it.

With that fact in mind I confidently went onto the military tour in Federal Republic of Germany. From there dark changes where a head in my life, I didn't see the storm that was brewing.

Right before leaving for Germany my wife was showing off, by fondling our oldest daughter and proclaiming how much the little girl like it. Given it would only be my word and without any hard proof I could not get any help, just a stern warning and lots of prayers to keep the girls safe. I know had something to worry about and nowhere to go and talk about it.

My unit was stationed in a quaint spa town with the Saline River running through it. Much of the city was on the rivers east bank and a large park and aeroplatt on the west side. There where ruins of roman watch towers on high hills on both sides of the river.

I would spend much of my off time just walking around the area and reading the historical marker that where over the place, including a number of mass graves from the many wars that had been fought there. I always carried a language book with me to help translate and by the time I left Germany I could read a German newspaper in less than a day. My hope was to encourage the girls to learn a foreign language as soon as they mastered the basic of English, once I got home.

Still much of that walking around was done in short day to day availability. Most of the six months there were either spent in the forward border camp, walking the East/West Germany Border around O.P. Serra, or at one of several training sites.

Had I brought my wife and the girls over it would had been very difficult for the family, most likely we would had to lived on the economy, in land were we did not speak, write, or even read the language and I would had been gone far more than I would had been home.

Since this tour was going to lead to the end of my enlistment, I started to look forward to coming home and going to school. There were my daily letters home, and a weekly telephone call I was always ensured that my wife and the girls were fine. We had friends and neighbors that said they were willing to support the home front, while I was away.

Shortly after our second daughter was born things quickly changed, I was rushed home by the army hospital, turned out my wife became a threat to the girls and herself. She had alienated our support structure and started to become violent.

Once I made it back to Ft. Sill things quieted down, but it wouldn't be until many years later that I found out what had fully happen, much of the actual information of my hardship discharge was reported without my knowing.

I would get my complete military record 10 years after the Termination of Parental Rights hearing with a note stating, "Do not release to service member." Then the dark story unfolded

It took over three months to complete the discharge and to come home 6 months earlier than planned. Still counting on what was promised to be waiting for me once I got home.

However once I got home everything had changed. Since this discharge was mostly unplanned I had to catch up with the developing needs. First we tried to store our belongings on one of the family farms in south central Wisconsin. The farm was in retirement and the many sheds were now empty.

Then a cousin's barn burnt down, with most of the livestock save, he needed a place to winter the animals and quick so all building were brought back to their purpose. Our belongings were now stuck in storage.

Our first plan was to let my family stay with a relative while I went back to Minnesota to find work and an apartment. The job was actually quick to find with a school bus driver for a local school bus service.

I was getting ready to start training when I had to go to Chicago, were the family ended up at a one of my wives' cousin house there. I can't remember taking her and the girls there and I think her cousin actually picked them from my family farm in Wisconsin

Still I do remember a sleepy drive on a cold Friday night to go pick them up, my wife had worn out her welcome in two places in less than two weeks. Once I got her and the girls back to Minnesota we used emergency assistance to help get an apartment so I could start work.

Once we moved into a local apartment I reported back to the fire department only to be denied the slot that was in reserve prior to my military leave. A very important promise was broken.

Since the fire department was a volunteer fire department, Department of Labor would not get involved, even though this would lock me out of my career field and had a negative effect to our marriage. By the fire department breaking their word, my wife questioned the value of my word.

There was a new fire chief voted in, his first action was to cancel the youth program that was working to well for the department, as well as remove 20 fire fighter positions as a cost saving measure. In little over a year several of the former youth members would sue for the positions we had been promised, but by then I had a much larger problem to deal with.

The school bus got us to the summer and I needed to find work to keep the family fed. I had also work at local fast food restaurant to have enough cash to take care of the family.

My EMT registry landed me a job with a local ambulance company that was short lived; part was a mistake I made taking the turn off Hamline Avenue exit from Highway 36. The other reason was not fitting in with some of the co-workers who were full-time fire fighters. I wasn't called in to be counseled, just dropped from the roster and sent home.

We were evicted after our oldest daughter was found trapped on the balcony. There were complaints to the landlord that we were fighting too much, which was daily now, nothing was going in our favor and something was going wrong. I didn't even feel like I was home. So we left my home town and hope for a better go at life, we didn't know that we had not hit bottom yet.

Next job would be with a pizza delivery chain. My wife at this time had taken a job at a nursing home in St. Paul, and by September we would move to suburb north of St. Paul. My attempt to join the fire department there failed as well, the fire chief told me that I **"Unsuitable because I was too eager."**

In the spring of 1984 the door of the car fell off, we went and got a newer car. Now payments were going to go on longer that our incomes would allow. With the move to Maplewood I was closer to work, but my hours got longer once I tried being an assistant manager.

Also in spring of 1985 my wives parents would file for divorce. This was the point where her anger at life began to show. She increased in her demands that **"If she felt like it, I would never see my girls for the rest of my life, if she ever decided to divorce."** She complained of how unfair it was for her mom and dad to wait until her youngest brother turned 18 and graduated from high school.**"Dad's should be paying until they are broke and with their lives."** I didn't realize how mad she really was until what happened next.

Pizza Delivery was at least stable but management at times was abusive. The action of my store manager compounded the abusive relationship that was occurring at home.

My wife was fired for assaulting a resident at the nursing home and took a new job at another nursing home again as an aid. She also went to the Army Reserves. We had agreed if we didn't get our finances to work out right by summer of 1985 she would go back to active duty, since my hardship discharge had made it impossible for me to return to active duty.

The plan didn't work, she was having serious problems and

by September 1985 she would be forced out of the reserves and barred from re-enlistment. She did try to transfer to a medical unit, the recruiter took me instead. I was back in the military as a medic in the Army Reserve.

Our oldest daughter at this time was a Houdini. I was always amazed at her ability to problem solve, but she always seemed to find ways that trapped her too. Like the night when we lived in back in the first apartment, she had trapped herself on our balcony. Now she would be found running in the hallway. I tried a suggestion out of the 14th edition of the Merck Manual for children with issues with night awaking.

Trying to keep the girls safe, I instead gave everyone something to use against me, something that would be hidden in the papers and never brought out into open court or questioned about. I was never question about the incident as well, no one spoke of it including my court appointed attorney.

During this turbulent time, my high school friend Pat came home from the Marine Corps. He stayed with us for a couple of weeks when he caught my wife attacking our youngest; I had seen the developing burses and an unexplained burn to the hand. Now with evidence maybe help would come?

When Pat witnessed the assault he made a report to the police. I was at work at the time of the incident, a police detective had contact me and gave me the news. As well as question about all the arguing between us that the neighbors were reporting.

During the month and a half the girls where in foster care we tried counseling, but it should had been individual rather than couple. I was being blamed for everything, the marriage became an issue of me forcing her and the children became unwanted by her, and the move to Minnesota I apparently didn't discuss with her. I was now the ultimate bad guy insensitive to the needs of a woman and abuse tyrant.

At this time I had put in an application for an ambulance service in San Diego, but she refused to make the move repeating her claim of **"Too many blacks and wetbacks there for her to move back to Southern California."**

During counseling and anytime I tried to speak I was cut off and only **"My wife was important, I was not."** The social worker from county social services was the same way. She showed up at our apartment only to talk to her, the county had nothing to do with fathers. We were simply obsolete and no longer a need to the family.

She was coaching my wife in ways the county could help remove me so she could give the girls up, if she ever felt the need. The more my wife pressed the county worker the less I was allowed into the meeting. Each time she came over, it ended with me in the kitchen over hearing their plot.

The county would help her achieve her goal of ridding her of family and of a no account husband. I didn't count in their eyes at all. The girls would remain in foster care for six weeks as we all waited for my wife to want them back.

The funny thing was for six weeks our arguments neither were almost non-existent, nor were there any of the treats of taking away my rights to the girls.

At no time, even to this period of time did my wife express any desire to divorce. Still there was the threat of the loss of my parental rights if she would ever desire such a course of action.

During that six week time count y social services never set up any other services, no parenting classes, no counseling, and no parenting evaluations. The only thing that would happen would be weekly visits from social worker, to plan and plot. The only other counseling we ever did was on our own and was too costly to continue.

Toward the end of August 1985 the girls would come home. Shortly afterwards we got an eviction notice from our landlord and I began looking for a new home to move to.

My wife had been working nights at a nursing home on the east side of St. Paul, she had lost her driver's license due to a hit and run accident she had caused shortly before our girls were sent to foster care. I had to get an old van, since hit and run accidents pull the plates off the car as well.

Shortly after the girls came home she took off with the van to get food for the home. Running a stop sign she was caught by the police; the van and food were impounded.

I had asked for a one hour nap since I had been working overnight and then I would have taken us to the store. She had gotten impatient and left the girls while I was sleeping.

She didn't call from the county jail were she was booked, and I was at home with the girls with no idea what had happened. Not that I could do anything, we only had money for a one way trip with a cab. I had no idea were either her or the van was until she got home, later that afternoon.

I had been working the evening shift, a co-worker of her would take her to work while I came home. I had left the pizza delivery job and took an assistant manager's job at a gas station. The problem was on the day the van was impounded I had walked the 7 miles to the lot only to discover I had left my wallet at home. I was running late for work, the food was getting heated by sun and God knows what she was doing to the girls.

Too many worries now ran through my head. I was able though to have a Police Officer verify my driver license and I got the food home, went to work only to be fired. So we decided to get the move done first then I would look for work again.

I had found a duplex in further north. Everything would be close, but my wife had given up, getting the down payment from her was like pulling eye teeth. As I started to pack things she started getting violent.

During an argument of the down payment for the new address our oldest fell in the bathtub knocking her two front teeth out. I could hear her whimpering and went to the bathroom to check.

She was holding a towel to her mouth and it was covered with blood. While I was assessing the injuries, my wife drained the tub even as I told her not too; the teeth were flushed down the drain.

Then she refused to let me take our daughter to the hospital until after a good outfit was put on. Our oldest was a champ at the hospital she let the doctors and nurses check her out. At times I don't know who was showing the bravest face, me for my daughter, or my daughter for me.

A week later our youngest chasing after her sister slipped and fell against the coffee table. Requiring stitches I took her to the same emergency room that I took our other daughter to a week earlier.

This time it was a harder job, our youngest fought the whole time, even in the papoose. Though I stayed at her side a tried to comfort her, it was a huge challenge. I didn't know I was on my final week with my girls. My wife had been preparing her move.

This last week was spent moving to the new home. I would do one trip during the day and one at night when I dropped my wife off for work. As the week progressed she became very hostile, and did not assist with the move at all.

Granted she was working nights and the move had to work around her sleep, however the one time I really needed her help, she first complained that she wish I was dead, then she tried to push me down the stairs as we moved the sofa. She got mad at the fact that I didn't get injured leaving me to load the heavy sofa into the van on my own.

I got more help from the girls and we made it such a game of it. When we were not packing I had cut up some grocery bags and we were practicing the ABC's and the 123's. At one point our oldest got into my army medical kit and pulled out my opthalamscope, and excitedly proclaimed, **"Let me see, let me see."** Then she started to look in my eyes. For the first time in a long time, I was spending full undivided attention with the girls.

If everyone would had let me I would had rather been a

house husband than what did happen the following week. I was having the time of my life with the girls.

By this time too many people from media outlets to county social services that would encourage women to go after their husbands with any weapon they could find. The belief that women are so passive that they have to be forced into an act of violence, while men enjoy being violent. Part of the theory was if the guy defends himself in an attack by his wife, then he is most likely guilty of abuse. **"Only an abusive person would use force against deadly force."**

Friday came; we attempted to get pictures of the girls. Our youngest was having separation issues which my wife interfered with the studio staff so only oldest daughter got her picture taken.

As we walked out of the local shopping mall, my wife began to threaten another woman who was bringing her boys to the mall. She started calling the woman a whore and even attempted to attack this unknown person. I wiggled in between the two women, who by now are both ready to fight each other and the kids and forced the still screaming wife of mine out the door with the girls in tow.

The rest of the weekend was rough, the move, my wife's out bursts was increasing and with no help in sight. The quote from social services hotline was **"If you're women we have plenty of help for you. But since your guy if you can't figure out your own problem, what makes you think we're going to do anything for you?"**

The girls and I had just dropped another load off at the new apartment. This was the downstairs of a two floor duplex. It was getting late and then furnace stopped working. It got cold and the girls and I bundled up and crawled together to keep warm.

By Monday I may had a total of 12 hours of sleep since Friday morning. Still in the old fashion I drove on, it was the 30th we needed to be completely moved out by noon. First thing I did when we woke up was to call the landlord about the furnace and pick up my wife from work. Once we departed her work, she was very agitated. She didn't like the idea we were moving and became very combative to the ride home.

She became violent when I informed her that most of the food had been moved over night and we only had two loads left. Next thing I knew my tools were bouncing off the dash board of the van as was headed down the street and the old apartment.

My wife had at one point attempted to jump out of the back of the van while I was doing about 40 mph, I had never seen her so wild, and we all were getting scared. When she emptied the tool box one of the wenches just barely missed our oldest daughters head as my wife threw the tools at me. I focused on the drive home. Once we got to the apartment she had a court appearance for the driving with a revoked license and I got the second to the last load done.

The telephone was shut off at the apartment and turned on at the duplex. While I was at the duplex I called county social services and mental health office looking for help. The only thing I got was the intake time for mental health walk in, nothing else was listened to, including my fears for my daughters and me. Not even a suggestion of making a police report came from the county, **"They are there to protect the women, only."** I was also told **"You just need to stop arguing with your wife and to stop fighting with her."** So nothing more could be done, the ideas were casted in concrete, **"It's the man's fault, period."**

While my wife threw her violent fit, I had thought about pulling up to a police station thoughts entered my mind.

1. Would it make her more agitated and even more violent?
2. Would the police believe enough to take the report?
3. Would I find help?

By the afternoon I found the answers were, Yes (and it would had endangered the girls even more) and no (the policy at this time made nearly impossible to make a report without definitive proof i.e. her actions had to have caused me to have an accident first and again no help was designed to help a father caught in this situation.

I had to be lying about my action and First Call for help were more concern if I was abusing my wife, **"Since women do not abuse people only men abuse"**.)

I could not do anything, but pray. My words alone would not get help to our door.

It started to rain and it was time to get the last load. Before we parted I had asked my wife if she got back in time from court to start loading the final items in the car so we could clear the apartment in time. At the time to return to our old apartment our youngest daughter could not find her shoes.

The van was warm and dry and pulled up to the back door so she never step foot in any puddle, she was light and easy to carry. Her feet never touch the ground.

Granted we all were tired. My wife was sleep on the floor of the old apartment, and when I woke her up she charged at me. She took me by surprise as she lifted me off the floor and carried me across the kitchen. As she slammed me into the wall she grabbed a butcher knife that was half sticking out of a box that was in the kitchen and was trying to slash me in the gut.

I did all I could to hold her back the only thing I could get a hold of was her hair, pulling her head down and pushing her as far away as possible; to reduce the chance she could see an point to aim the knife at. Her blind swinging of the knife was just barely missing me. All a long she was telling that she wanted me dead, that she was going to kill me. Her actions were supporting her words.

I am begging, pleading for not only my life but the girls as well. If I didn't we all would had died September 30th 1985. I was losing ground both with the pleading and the self defense, I didn't want to strike back, but I had no other choice. I have spent the better half of the past 20 years trying to replay what I could have done better. Had I knew what was happening was schopherina, I would have known I was in even more danger than anyone would have ever believed.

I have always been taught to escalate only to the point to stop an assault, as a medic I had found myself in situation were a Greco-roman wrestling move had work as well as talking the patient through to the point they stopped fighting. This time was different, the threat of death was real and unending, to both the girls and myself. She was going to free herself from the lot of us, and she was showing no signs of stopping and I am being held against a wall, in a small corner with a knife that is just missing my shirt. I had no ability to gain control over her and stop the wild swings of the knife. Nothing was working.

I was not going hold out too much longer; I was being forced to fight back. It only took three taps, like a knock to a door, to get her to drop the knife, I had lost count to the blows that I took as she tried to break me grip and close in those few inches of air between the knife blade and my skin. The saving grace was that her knife swings where as wild and blind as she was throwing the tools. I had simply tapped her on the only part of her body I could reach and had control of, just to get her to drop the knife.

I had tools in my back pocket to dismantle the table, never thought to use any of them anyways, I had been too busy try to talk her out of the fight, but she not stopping, she only wanted me dead. Then the fight stopped and county policy took over and the hell of 20+ years had its birth.

My wife last words to me were; **"Now I can keep you from ever seeing the girls ever again. You will die without ever seeing your precious daughters."** The plot that was planned the month prior begun, she slammed the knife down and walked out the door. I checked on the girls who were waiting crying in the living room, I touched nothing.

Knowing the cops were probably coming I kept the evidence in place. We both had gone through army basic training, she had just as much ability to fight as I had, but none of that would ever be looked at. At least 6 sirens could be heard outside heading in my direction.

I met the first cop on the stairs the second one grabbed the girls and took shelter in a downstairs apartment, of a gal who would only talk to us once and only on that very day but would give testimony to anything my wife claimed as if the neighbor had directly witnessed, even though the neighbor never stepped foot in our apartment for the whole year we had lived there.

The police officer and I where calmly talking, I was able to tell him my side of the story. Still, though I would not be allowed to make a police report for the events leading up to their summons to our address.

However his supervisor blasted into the scene with such profanity it would have made my drill sergeant blush. I was to be immediately handcuffed and "**You show him how Pieces of $#!* are treated**". The cop tried to plead my case that something wasn't adding up. The police sergeant threatened his job right on the spot, "**No cop is to take any statement from a father. The policy is women are the victims and men are the problem, nothing a father has to say is to be taken seriously because we are the ones trying to hide something.**"

He looked at me and I simply turned around and felt the handcuffs tighten around my wrists. As we walked out to the squad car he told me he was sorry, he had no choice. I knew the policy myself the last few years as this policy was being developed I knew the flaw well; nobody would take the time to ask one simple question. He left me in the squad car alone while the scene played out, my set of tools still in my back pocket, I wasn't a threat. I was never brought in to be book and was never charged with any crime.

The fact still remained we were evicted and were now almost two hours overdue the move. My wife never pressed charges which would have caused an investigation. At this time women were encouraged not to press charges; social services had a better idea in getting around the investigative process and meet the needs of the "policy".

After about 45 minutes I was released, and threaten of being ran into jail if I ever showed my face in the city again by the police supervisor and the cop that had first arrived watched me as I loaded the final belonging in the van and drove away.

I would not sleep for over a week, mainly cried in my daughter's new bedroom, the beds were made and their toys were waiting for them. I shook from the pain of what had just happened. I would never be allowed or offered the chance to make my own report, **"Men are lairs anyways, and why would you expect us to waste the paper?"**

Within two days a county deputy would show up at my door, it was the summons for the domestic relations court hearing. I had spent about three nights pouring over the law books and trying to find an attorney that would represent a father.

The law was clear; it would be a challenge to deny my parental rights, if the county would follow have the requirements of the law. What I didn't count on was a little knows ideology had been developing called agency law. Agency Law is set by the policy of a given government agency and gave an ability to forbade the written law and accomplish a given policy ideology. This process occurs without the legislative process and without public hearing.

Ideally by constitutional mandate, the states cannot make laws that supersede the federal code; however the states can make laws that are stricter than the federal code. Agency law becomes its own set of rules; often deny the basic premises of the law to allow the given agency the freedom to do its own thing and enforce the agencies ideology beyond the protection of the law and constitution of the people.

I was counting on what I read both by federal code and by state of Minnesota to be followed, what happened next was neither, it wasn't even close.

On the day of domestic relation court hearing no other representative, be it police or county social service would speak to me. Women Advocate's Attorney was provider for my wife, I could not only afford one I could find none to represent me.

No attorney would represent me unless I could come up with $10,000.00 first, right off the bat I was being advised to simply **"Quit this worthless fight. Besides the county does not have to nor will respect the rights of fathers. If your wife wants to give the girls up then it is our obligation to make it happen. No matter how good the father may think he is. Fathers don't count in our eyes or courtrooms"** I also learned that many attorneys refused to represent fathers because it was career suicide for the any attorney and was viewed as the attorney supporting domestic violence and child abuse.

The judge first appeared that he was willing to listen to both sides, however I was called a lair for bring up the knife attack and the only thing he cared about was did I hit her, not for any reason why. Didn't matter that there were no injuries, no bruises, no charges all that mattered was did I hit her? That was all he needed to know.

A visitation plan was also to be set up and I was given a telephone number to call to arrange visits with my daughters as all the papers were getting together one of the clerks would say to me **"Sure women are abusive, sometimes. But men are more the problem anyways and until we can get you men under control, only then will we stop domestic violence and child abuse."**

I was ordered to a 4 hour anger management course ran by a charity social foundation. It was a male bashing session of epic proportions, **"Men enjoy beating their women for all sorts of reasons, and the steak was too cold, when he wanted fish. Even simply for the fun of it. Let's face it men enjoy being violent"** I attempted to talk about what I had just gone through and was told to face the facts **"Men enjoyed beating women, so don't feeds us the bullshit you where abused by her, we know that never happens. Women don't even want to be violent, that is only a male thing."**

Trying to set up my visit with my daughters became the

next horrid experience. I had called that number, only to be forwarded to another number, then another, yet another. In fact I was on the telephone for 6 hours and not once was able to talk to anyone one, nor set up my visit with my girls. Because of the nightmares of that final fight with my wife I was very concern of the safety of my daughters, I tried to find the investigator for this case as well. I went to the county social services directly.

It became a weekly trip, either by the daily attempts on the telephone or the two to three times a week that I was passed from one office to the next. It didn't matter no one would talk to a father for any reasons. **"Fathers aren't the worth of the waste of taxpayer's money. And (I) was out for a rude awakening."**

I drew bus tokens from the receptionists' desk when I took the bus, since I couldn't afford the gas for work and all these other trips.

Within two weeks I got summons for Child Support Collections.

I was working at the time for a security firm and had been given the assignment to guard a house in a western suburb, owned by a popular rock star. It was for a measly $3.75 an hour. I would also be assigned to do night watch at certain over night restaurants located throughout the Twin Cities, often in crime ridden neighborhoods.

That income plus reserve drills gave me roughly $800.00 a month to live on after taxes.

The child support was planned to an imaginary potential of $1,200.00 a month and I was to pay $189.00 each month **"Before I found a place to sleep, food to eat, or fuel to get to work."** I countered that I would starve to death the cold reply was, **"Good, then that will solve the problem."**

I was simply shown the door, not even given the address where I was to send the funds, just shown the door. I started taking the paperwork to our state capital. I used what my dad left behind, knowledge of the system and the fact that all of us can have our voice at least at the marble steps of our state capital.

I didn't realize that I was going to be for such a long time a single voice, when we would look over the paperwork my state representative shuttered, but always ensure that the courts would sort it out. It wasn't the job of the legislators or the governor to challenge the courts. I had found another dead-end, but at least they would take the time to listen, the one thing the courts wouldn't do.

Still, I was advised to keep my representative posted, by the time I would go through this mess it would involve over a dozen state representatives and senators, all shock at what would happen as well as the why. It wasn't that the laws were bad or poorly written, our counties had simply exempted themselves from following the law, and agency policy prevailed.

The stress of not being able to pay my child support, as well as not being allowed to see my girls were taking the huge toll on me, I entered a period of distress, becoming unable to focus and stay motivated to day to day living.

Meanwhile back at the rock star's house I posted my old blue van at the end of the driveway and directed his fans away. During the winter his brother often came by the house. We almost had a game going on. Because my tires were bad the van often got stuck at the foot of the driveway and his brother's light little Honda kept getting stuck by the garage. We had often pushed each other out of the snow that winter.

By spring I went back to the pizza delivery service since I couldn't afford the cost of gas, the apartment or the child support.

About 4 months into this period I stumbled into the very office that I was to call and set up my visits, as well as the office I was to pay child support too as well. These two offices were hidden in another building that the county leased and would be difficult to find even with directions. It was simply on a day that I had walked around to the different county offices that I noticed this back hallway to an elevator that led my there, felt like I was in a **"Get Smart"** TV show episode.

I had just applied for bankruptcy and had become homeless,

unable to keep the two bedroom apartment anymore. Our belongings I put in storage. I started to live either out of my mom's basement or the back of my van.

I had also started college at the University of Minnesota, Twin Cities Campus. It would take 3 weeks to set up my first visit with my daughters.

My wife was constantly obstructing the chance for visitation every turn of the way, first the visits needed to be supervised by her request, then she wanted my brother Jim to be the supervisor, he was 15 at the moment and had no means to drive to pick up the girls' for visits.

It went on and on. On the day I was finally able to have four hours with my daughters, my wife would turn the girls over to the county one final time. She made it clear, **"The county was to find a way to remove my rights, so she could give up hers."** Now the social service had the desired mission, was the only mission the county wanted, give mom what she wanted, to heck with the dad. **"It's not like the father's feelings really matter that much anyways."**

My next visit would be a parenting evaluation, the only one conducted by an outside agency that ceased to exist shortly afterwards for unknown reasons. The quote for the evaluation was **"Although the relationship between father and his daughters is appropriate and nurturing, it is our desire that Termination of Parental Rights be followed through."**

Back at reserve drill a member from my unit who was a social worker from Wisconsin claimed **"Why should the county waste money supporting a single father. We can pay people to be a better parent than what we would waste trying to teach a father to be a good parent."** What I felt in my stomach was the deep burn of betrayal. No where could I to for real support or understanding.

Everywhere I went I was told that I was being selfish, because **"Men only want sex so stop being so phony in claiming that you really do care about your children. If you really are caring about your kids you would be trying to get a**

$50,000.00 a year career and if you can't find one, do the right thing and give your girls up."

At the University I had met a young woman that had treated me better than anyone had ever before. I was human again, not riff raff, not a piece of trash. Roxanna and I never came to a complete relationship other than solid friends; she became to me the kid sister I never had. As our lives developed we have always stayed in contact. She was calm in a very bitter storm.

The clinic that which conducted the parenting evaluation used this relationship as a means to take a stance against my parental rights. Nick, as she likes to be called, was too young and too beautiful in their eyes for me to be hanging around the likes of me.

The county social worker then started to harass me over the same. What I find funny is during this time period it was encouraged for fathers to quickly find another woman in their life so the county could give the kids to the "New" mother.

The social worker even asked how it was like to have sex with her, calling me a liar for never being able to have such a relationship, part was the fact that the stress of what I was being sent through made me impotent.

But that wasn't what was happening here; Nick brought me back to humanity. Not to become the "New" mother just a lifelong friendship built along the way. I believe this friendship is what allowed for a successful marriage later on.

In time we would part with our spouses, but still with connection that is still as strong today as any of the past 23 years could bring, a sister that I have loved for the first day our eyes met.

MEETING THE SOCIAL WORKER

By now my telephone days had gone on for about 5 months, with the girls now back in foster care I was direct to call one of the first numbers I would dial in the weekly telephone tag. I would be transferred to the social worker who had all along been assigned to the case.

We would meet for the first time at a McDonalds, just blocks from the foster home were the girls at in July '85 when my wife was caught assaulting our youngest. He presented papers for me to sign.

He told me; **"It is worthless to fight and the county does not have to, nor will ever give fathers any equal chance at parenting. You need to see that giving the girls up are the only thing that you could ever do right for your girls and in your life. You are a waste to this society, and as much of a waste for your girls. If you sign these papers your nightmare will end. Otherwise I will make you wish you were never born and the courts will see the waste of life that you are."**

The papers were to voluntary give up my parental rights, fully against the US Code and Minnesota State Laws that prohibit such interactions by county officials to coerce an adoption. The only things missing were my signature, it was already predated. I refused to sign. I was then made to pay for the parenting evaluation.

When I brought the payment for the parenting evaluation I was to report to the very receptionist desk I drew the bus tokens from. It was the social workers assigned reception desk all along.

The next thing I would learn is that; **"It doesn't matter what any of these people tell you. You're nothing but a worthless biological parent. You have no voice, you have no choice, it doesn't matter what you accuse the county of doing. The social workers word will always be viewed as the truth, no matter what. You really think that being a father really means anything to anyone anymore?"**

Within the week the Roman Catholic Church would close its doors to me as well, I was truly alone and nowhere to go. I had called the social services hot line, explained my situation and was told; **"I am so sorry, but if you were a woman we have plenty of places for you to go. But since you're a guy, you just need to buck up and take it like a man. Men are not worth the services. Besides it would be such a waste of money anyway. Our recommendation is that you do whatever the county tells you to do and you will be able to have the freedom to do whatever it is with your life.**

I had even went to the State Human Rights office just to be told; **"Caucasian men are the problem, not the ones with the problem. Do yourself the favor and stop being such a worthless bum that you are and do what social services wants you to do. Your children really would be better without you."**

While going to school I had pitched a camp within some trees between the University of Minnesota, Twin Cities Campus and its sports compound, in between train tracks that led to the Dinkytown area. I kept a clean and disguised camp and for a Hobo I was doing very well. Since I had some medical knowledge some of the other transients would turn to me for minor medical help it wasn't much, but it help create an air of belonging to those in the area.

A property owner in the area had an abandoned grain elevator, what was freaky was the fact that my initials where spray painted to the side of one of the silos, long before I even knew of this place, must had been an omen. The gentleman who owned the property was allowing it to be used as a jungle camp for the transients. One individual who everyone knew as Irish was the lead on the property; he was given an old camper and the keys to the building so we could have electricity and water if we wanted. There were several semi trailers and thousands of old pallets in piles in and around the place; it was a fire waiting to happen.

One morning I woke to screams and barking dogs. Three squad cars of police had raided the camp and beating on Irish, the Rodney King beating was minor compared to what I had witnessed. They cleared the camp with such a display of violence it was sickening. After the last of the hobos where led off they bragged amongst themselves of the fun they had on their frolic and how they would such book the lot for resisting arrest no one will know truth, they just needed someone to beat up that night.

I close enough to hear their voices and see their faces, yet camouflaged enough not to be seen. I was in total fear until the last police car left. It was time to find a place to call home. Two days later everyone returned to the camp telling of their time in the city jail. Nearly ten years later one of the police officers was fired for brutality in another case, his face was that of what I saw laughing under the street lamp that brutal night.

The first review hearing would not occur until October 1986, 13 months after this whole nightmare began. I was finally appointed an attorney. On the day of the first review and only 40 minutes before we were to convene before judge, we finally spoke. I wasn't even allowed to say much I was cut off by my attorney and was told; **"You're getting what every man deserves and you better get used to it."** To say I was stunned was an understatement; I attempted to ask for a different attorney and was never heard or allowed by the county courts.

The judge asked a few questions and got some very poor answers from everyone between the county and the attorneys. He was very angered at what was appearing to be some mismanagement. I would be allowed two weekly visits with my daughters, parenting classes; I was to call the social worker every working day and another review was set in 6 months.

By now the van had dead, no longer running. I had received assistance in Hennepin County for housing with the upcoming winter. It was a studio apartment at a price I could afford. When the social worker stopped by for housing review he yelled at me; **"You selfish pig what makes you think I should allow you to have visits here. Until you have a deluxe two bedroom apartment I will never advocate any at home visits with you and your girls. I again remind you that surrendering your parental rights are the only option we want you to do. So get it out of your head that you have equal rights for your children."**

I had been riding a bicycle from the heart of Minneapolis to the foster home, 15 miles one way. No parenting class referral came from the social worker, I had to find a course on my own, and all with all the looking I was not finding one acceptable to social worker.

Instead the daily phone calls became calls to surrender my parental rights and other verbal harassment meant to force me to quit the **"Worthless fight and give up my parental rights as the only reasonable way out."**

I had purchased a used pick-up truck that truly on its last days with what little money I had left with my student loan money. It was constantly breaking down as well. So the bike was always a back up. Often it was my only means of transportation other than walking. By now I had been walking nearly 10 miles a day, and each month would have a walk between 20 and 40 miles which help cool some of the stress I was feeling.

By Christmas I was a total wreck and couldn't stand it anymore. Halloween of 1986 would be the last holiday I would ever have with my daughters. Nick and I took the girls trick and treating, made them up in costumes and we had a great time. However the girls themselves had difficulties with the trauma that all this separation was causing and my oldest daughter had an allergic reaction to the makeup.

The foster mother would tell me at the next visit; **"Neither you or your wife will ever be allowed a visit during a holiday again. These are no longer your girls and they need to spend it with their real family. Besides why did you use makeup that you knew your daughter was allergic to?"**

I was crushed, first this was the only time I would take the girls trick or treating, my wife wouldn't let us do it before.

By 1985 my wife had already removed the girls from my reach. I didn't know that our oldest daughter was sensitive to the store makeup. But there was no way to argue the truth, by now I wasn't looked at as a source of truth anyways. Not that the truth really matter at this point.

After taking the girls out on Halloween Nick and I drove the truck to Duluth and spent the rest of the weekend together. She had a friend taking college up there and we spent some time with her as well. On the return the truck would break down and I never could get it to work ever again.

I started failing at school, trouble bled over into work, I was starting to fall apart and there was nowhere I could go for help. The mental health workers in Hennepin County wanted to put me on drugs with a flowery speech about how great life is being medicated. All I wanted was my kids in my life, not have them be used as a weapon against me.

Then the job market collapsed in Minnesota, search through some newspapers at a library at the University I spotted the help wanted pages for Los Angeles, both Marianne and Sue were from there. With my wife never wanting to go back, I needed work, and I would hop on a freight train to try to create a new start.

I underestimated how long this trip would take. I planned five days, it took almost two weeks. I would reach LA in the New Year; I had Christmas in Spokane, Washington.

JAM

I had run out of food just on the first leg. Recharged at the Salvation Army, and prepared to lie down for the night.

Two couples would appear asking if there where anyone there that would like a homemade Christmas Diner, six of us would get into their car and travel, to the east side of Spokane for a full meal and Caroling. It was fun and a fond memory of even in the darkest time God has ways of showing his light.

While there I met another fellow traveler, he was making his rounds, having given up on what society has to offer he had taken to the rails and knew them well. By now I don't even remember his name , but what I do remember is his telling me that for five years he had rode the rails collecting county checks from Minneapolis, Eugene, and LA. That was the only way he could make it. By riding the rails he made over $2000.00 a month, only LA required he stayed long enough for work. But even then that was for one week then off on the rails he would go again, collecting welfare checks along the way and staying a day or two in county shelters as a bed to sleep on.

In my backpack I kept a copy of all my training documents and a suit to look for work in, which remained protected and ready. By the time I reached my last stop I was almost out of food, only one meal was left and a long walk was beginning.

The train was broken apart in Van Nyes, at the Budweiser Plant of all places. My walk would end in Long Beach by the pier. First I had to find my bearings and figure out where I was going. I had a choice, go to the freeway ramp and thumb a ride or walk. I never really liked hitchhiking and I love to walk. I just didn't know I was going to do nearly 80 miles within one 24 hour period and without any food.

The walk was actually quite refreshing. Up to now I had been walking and biking all over Minneapolis and St. Paul so the long walk was totally prepared for. It is just LA really isn't set up for walkers.

As I headed south I climb over the San Monica Mountains, with all the housing developments I had paved streets to walk on and most residents either had a brick fence or shrubs all the way to the curb line. There was no sidewalk to walk on. It really wasn't a problem until I started my descent, on the climb there was hardly any traffic. As I got closer to Sunset Boulevard the traffic picked up. A motor cycle cop cruising by yelled at me to get off the street, but where was I to walk? He kept on going, never to stop.

I came across Sunset Ave and I walked across a college campus, I don't remember which one it was; on the other side was a bustling city strip of store, shops, traffic and people. I got bumped by a man pushing a shopping cart who started screaming; **"I'll sue you, I'll sue you."** I kept on my path.

I reached Pacific Coast Highway as the sun was beginning to set, I would follow it all the way to Long Beach taking much of the night to get there. I raided a pizza parlor dumpster for something to eat, usually the freshest food was on the top and I didn't have to dig, I just needed something to eat. A lesson I had learned by another homeless gent back in Minneapolis. Water was plentiful with faucets and fountains everywhere to be seen.

Shortly before reaching the airport I found an abandoned shopping cart sitting in the street. I noted the name of the store on the cart and look around to see if there was a sign in sight to be returned too. There were none, by now my left knee was hurting from all the walking. I had injured it while I was at Fort Sill, twisting it on a stairwell as a group of us carried a soldier down a narrow set of stairs. This happen within the month leading to my departure for Germany and up to now never had been a problem. The decent down the mountain had inflamed it though and I was in quite a bit of pain. The cart brought a much needed break from the back pack.

With me I had a maple shaft that I had recovered from Minneapolis, it was a tree that had been planted and then destroyed when a car had hit it removing it from its trunk.

I had peeled off the bark and trimmed off the branches, it was at the prefect height.

But on this night even it was failing to help balance the load from the pain in my knee, so in the cart it went as well.

I almost made from the airport through Hermosa Beach when a squad would pull up. First I had a weapon, (the staff), then I wasn't a legal California resident (since I obviously was a vagabond by my dress). He was reaching for something to run me in for.

I was wearing my old army field jacket that had my National Registry of Emergency Medical Technician Patch sewn to it. I kept the patch turned to him as he made me abandon the cart and the staff. I was to just leave "His Town" which was simply across the street.

I put my pack back on my back and continued walking; it was about 4am, I had been walking for 20 hours. I crossed the street into Torrence. I had a small hill to climb and on the reverse side saw the store that the cart came from simply a ¼ mile from where the only cop who would trouble me was. I had unknowingly been walking toward the store ever since I picked up the cart. My knee was really bothering me so I took a break at a bus stop.

There I met some people who gathering to catch a bus to work we got into a friendly conservation and I was given enough money to take the bus on the last 8 miles of the trip into Long Beach. I would get off the bus at the Long Beach Mall and gave Sue a surprising call.

We had reconnected just before Christmas and talked off and on throughout my trip to California. She knew I was coming, just didn't realize how close I really was until I was standing at her door. I was made immediately to take a shower and she washed my clothes. For the first time we actually made love to each other, but the pain of the rape was still haunting her. I stayed the weekend then went to county social services for assistance.

At the county social services office I would be handed cash (signed for $50.00, was given $6.00), food stamps (signed for $200.00, given $150), and bus tokens (signed for $10.00, given

$5.00). I was sent to the county shelter where I could; **"Use all the drugs and alcohol that I want. Oh if I complain that I was shorted on the amount I would be refused all services."** I told the young lady I was here to find work and that I didn't use drugs and was there to find money for booze, **"Sure, right that's what they all say."** was the reply.

I found work as a live in aid for a family that father was suffering Alzheimer's, had my own room. The effects of the past months were showing. My emotions were in total disarray. It was a good job and I got along well, but all the emotional abuse had made me restless. I was also under the pressure to develop into my own housing.

Some of the services, parenting classes and such that county back home wanted I tried to fulfill in L.A., but it was very unsuccessful. It seemed like everything was fine until anyone I talked to talked to the Minnesota social worker, then everything became unavailable again. It was a very visible pattern, it happened in Minnesota and it was happening again in L.A.

Shortly before the termination of parental rights trail the Minnesota social worker would admit he was putting people to pressure me to give up my parental rights rather than to succeed with any plan to be reunited with my daughters.

Prior to the home health job I had applied for a job at local hospital as transportation orderly. I was renting a room at a local hotel; things at least had a forward motion to it for once.

Maybe it was because I was free from all the abuse that Minnesota became, I was free from the abuses of my wife, the social worker and the court appointed attorney.

At no time did anyone want my story, because I was the birthfather my story could not possibly be true, I am just having it out against social workers and just need to do what I am being told; **"Give your girls up, you have no worth them anymore."**

MARCH 1987

The next review hearing was approaching I made my arrangements to be there, I had some vacation time and decided to take the Amtrack home. It was cheaper than the plane and gave me the opportunity to reflect. It is not a direct route from L.A. to Minneapolis and I found a trip that would take me to San Antonio and Chicago before arriving in Minneapolis. My return trip would almost mimic the freight train ride months earlier, just more comfortable.

While at the hearing the social worker was livid, I had, **"No right moving to California and screwing with his case."** I needed to: **"Give up, surrender your parental rights and return to Minnesota."** Luckily, the judge didn't agree with social workers ideology, he saw that I was trying to make things better. He also didn't agree with social workers visitation plan that was limited to one hour a week and tightly supervised. Neither was needed or very practical. I was to have once a month visit that would start out at four hours and grow as they succeeded.

The social worker agreed to a plan that would not interfere with weekends that I had military training, however on my return to L.A. I discovered that I wouldn't have the money for the plane trip I would miss the first visit. I had hope for the possibility of taking military Space Available flights as a means of affording the trips, but without transportation I could never get to an air force base to catch a flight.

May of 1987 was one of my best visits with my daughters, but then it would be the visit used the most against me. The weather was a sunny and warm 80+ degree day. My plan was to spend a little time with girls at the foster home then to take them out to a park and finally a trip to a McDonalds that was little more than a mile from the home.

But, I was short on cash, so the girls and I talk about it and the foster mother gave me a $20.00 bill to pay for the meal. It was a great time. We skipped rocks at a nearby pond and had nothing but care free fun with each other.

After the meal at McDonalds we stopped at a park and played some more. I took pictures of the girls on a playground set. We laughed and played and had a great time together. For the first time in nearly three years I felt like I had my family back.

Then the real problem begun, on the walk home the girls started talking and asking about us coming home together and why we couldn't be a family together.

At social worker's office I was chastised for answering their questions, for wrestling with them, for screwing up his case and not moving back to Minnesota, or surrendering my parental rights as his authority demanded. I started too talked to him about the June visit. I had annual training coming up and only one weekend in June would be open for me to visit the girls. The social worker would stall on the June visit, nothing would be agreed until after I returned to L.A.

What happened next was disgusting. The social worker offers me a six hour visit with my daughters as long as I would go AWOL from annual training, full custody would be guarantee if I simply desert the military altogether. He even admitted to the pressuring agencies I had tried to receive the required services from, having them withhold services and encourage evaluations that supported the termination of parental rights.

He stated that if I was to **"Go AWOL (he) would tell these other services to work with me rather than to push for the termination of my parental rights. If I was to desert all together then to work even closer to make a successful reunion, otherwise there will be hell to pay."**

During my May reserve drill I escaped three robbery attempts against me as I walked through downtown L.A. one was by knife point. I had transferred to the California Army National Guard. The medical unit was located in Long Beach so I had no more need to travel through L.A. bus system to get to drill. Besides the guard had more openings for the 91C (Practical Nurse) than reserves. The social worker declared the transfer as a means of dodging my parental responsibilities and a violation to the visitation agreement.

By July I was refused any additional visitation time with my daughters, the social worker gave me a grave warning. I had one chance to desert the military desert the military to prove I do indeed love my daughters. He promised me a make sure I had a fair chance of retaining my parental rights, if I didn't desert or surrender my parental rights; he would start the termination process immediately.

The shorten visit went well, though this time I was barred from leaving with the girls. They were in a respite home in North Saint Paul and he alerted the foster parent declaring me a runway threat and that I might to try running off with the girls. But the fight between the county and I was at its ugliest point. I requested a different social worker and was refused. I was told again that I needed to do what the social worker demanded me to do. This case was totally polarized and I was to carry the full blame for not being coopertive to the county.

I called mom as I waited at the airport she had some rough news for me, first a close cousin of mine was killed in England, his wife and children were killed as well. They were on their way to pick up his mom and dad at the Heathrow Airport, they were running late.

Marvin had passed a car and drove head onto a truck the

car was flatten, everyone was killed instantly. I never got to meet his wife and child; we were always in different parts of the world she was in the navy and I was struggling to bring my life around. The second thing I was told was that my wife had been harassing my family calling my mother and sister at all hours. When mom and Mary tried to report my wife to the county, Mary and Becky both were threaten to have their daycare services closed.

I had about two hours before the flight and Marvin and his families were just buried at Fort Snelling Cemetery, just a mile from where I was. I had the time, so I took the walk and found the grave that held them. It was another lonely flight.

By the time I got back to L.A. I was again an emotional wreck. What I did know was that I was going to have to get back to Minnesota and try to get this case over with. My wives harassment of my family was in fact too much and the counties abuse was getting to be too much. So I transferred to Minnesota and transferred to the National Guard. I was on my final visits with my daughters. By December I would have my last visit with my daughters. The Termination of Parental Rights hearing was in March 1988

Part of the visitation problem was the fact for work I had been medical support for some additional training opportunities. The social worker refused to schedule visits on weekends that I was available, only to continue his push of that I needed to desert the military in order to save my parental rights.

The guard was sending me to nursing school, a future that would allow me to support my children. The county offered nothing in comparison. We were in deadlock; the social worker had already started the process to end the existence of my family.

County officials made it very clear they would not allow me to have custody of my daughters and run off to Texas for school no matter what the army would provide along the way.

I had also made some connection with services in another county, finally got into a parenting class and attempt to work through that counties mental health for some services. At my appointment I talked about everything up to this point, my father's death, and the high school years on the fire department, and the things I witnessed working at Ft. Sill and the time spent with my wife.

During that visit the psychiatrist asked me **"What does it feel like to rape women?"** I asked him where he came up with that idea. He replied **"I feel it is very unlikely for any male to be a rape victim. I am more concerned about this woman you must have raped and the trouble you caused in her life than anything your current wife is putting you through, or is she the woman you raped?"** I never did convince him of what had happened in the barracks back in Fort Sill, he would never take any notes while I told the story.

My mom worked just down the hallway from the county Mental Health in another office. She would tell me how the psychologist questioned her over "my fantasy" of being on the fire department in high school. He would later write in his evaluation that I was in activities that were; **"Inappropriate for age"** in high school, I guess I was to smoke dope, drink beer, and chase skirt instead. Mom had told him it wasn't a fantasy I told him of the things I had done. In his eyes the services I did in high school made me unfit to be a parent.

That county finally set me up for parenting classes that social worker had me search for and the program wanted to do another parenting evaluation. But then he would not allow it. **"Those days were done. (I) needed to get on with my life without my daughters. (I) had wasted enough of their time and life."**

I was recorded as an alcoholic and abusive tyrant that only had my interest at heart, no care or feelings for my children. I was such a total failure unable to keep a job or a home. My involvement in the National Guard was a means to obstruct the visitation plan and was considered unlawful by the social worker. My rough housing with the girls was a sign that I was preparing them to be sexually abused in some future date.

I was abusive for giving my daughters a horsy back ride or tumbling with them.

The social worker would also report that the first five months of silence in this case was caused by the county not knowing my whereabouts, funny to think the county was able to deliver every summons without difficulty. He just never got out from behind his desk, not even to meet me in his waiting room. He even stated that I was a threat to his life; though his address and telephone number was available in the telephone book.

Nick was considered a whore in the social workers eyes and he asked what it was like to have sex with her, since she was so attractive it must be something else.

He pressed me to admit that I had sexual relationships with her, and called me a liar for claiming that we never did.

He did give me credit, for I had never changed my story even after the near 2 ½ years of emotional abuse that he put me under. But he warned me; **"The truth and facts doesn't matter in Child Protection, what only matters that we can trick the judge in signing away your parental rights. The truth and facts are not needed. As a father you can spend the rest of your life telling the truth, not even your daughters are ever going to listen to you. My title is my word and I (the social worker) can say anything I (the social worker) like"** He then went on; **"As far as I (the social worker) am concerned you are nothing but a worthless waste of time, life and air. You will never amount to anything important or worthwhile. Matter of fact since you lack the maturity to surrender your rights on my command, you need to find the courage to commit suicide. Since suicide would be the only thing of value you would ever do for your children."** He continued **"As far as I am concerned you can be a fire fighter, a nurse, #%%* you can even be a Boy Scout leader. In my opinion you have nothing to offer your daughters, so I am taking them away."**

Then he said something that to this day I find sickening in his belief of fatherhood he said; **"I believe your play with your children is an act of abuse. Since the only reason a father** wrestles with his children is to prepare the children for a future of sexual exploitation."

His comments were in regards to the tumbling, wrestling and horsey back rides I would give to my daughters and had always done with them ever since they learned to walk. It was the same activity rule appropriate by the only parenting evaluation early on in the case.

The trial was only a week away. At the hearing it was dismal, I was reported to the judge each agency that was represented made the same claimed as my; **"Actions no matter how appropriate were too little too late in efforts and that to strip my parental rights would be an error on the side of safety and that served in their eyes my daughters best interest." All reasonable efforts had been accomplished and termination way the only course of action desired or needed."**

I would be slammed for the visit in May for getting the girls dirty and it was testified that my youngest daughter was ill when we went out for our walk that day and that she was covered with mud. My attorney would only allow the picture of my girls skipping stones to the judge and not the picture on the play ground set that showed no mud on either girl.

Horsy back rides that I gave my girls became examples of what was declared as inappropriate rough housing and their difficulties when I left from my visits was a sure sign that I did not belong as their father. It was one slam after another, it almost seamed scripted at times each of the agencies represented said the same thing over and over again. **"No matter how successful I had been lately it was too little too late to be a value. It would be better to error on the side of safety in regards for the girls than to respect any rights a father."**

Since I was now making more money than minimum wage it was questionable is I was going to have a court appointed attorney or have to represent myself. This caused the case paperwork to be released to me prior to the trial, something that at the time was rarely done.

Behind the scenes the original judge was promoted to another office and a new judge was appointed to Child Protection. By default just the length of this case would justify the Termination of Parental Rights and nothing else was needed.

What was found in the paperwork was alarming. A detailed history of alcoholism was described, even though I had no arrests of any kind in my life and the only evidence they used was provided by what my wife would claim and what the different agencies that she talk to would support without any examination of me.

I also learned that in those first five months that no one in county wanted to talk to me, my girls spent four of them in foster care while my wife was admitted to the hospital for psychiatric problems; she had been diagnosed with several issues include manic depression and paranoid schizophrenia. The county no matter how hard I was trying to talk to social services, no one from any of the many offices would not take any effort to return the favor.

The assigned social worker declared that for the first five months he did not know where my where about were to justify the lack of earlier communications and the inappropriate run around that occurred during the first months of this nightmare. No regard that the county sheriff would always find me when the county services asked. It was just that the social worker never tried nor never left his office when I was standing at his receptionist desk.

One thing to note of the management of this case was the was the fact that for 2 and a half years I was only put under relentless force to simply surrender my parental rights, never to confess any wrong doing, nor was I ever presented with criminal charges of abuse or neglect. The only course of action taken was to press me into giving up on the idea of being a father of my daughters.

The social worker declared that my transfer to the California National Guard made the visitation agreement null and void since it was voluntary on my part for moving to California for work and it was I that polarized the case. How I flaunted his authority and failed to follow his orders, how selfish I was for simply not giving up. I never saw so many people in my life testifying in the counties behalf, for what they called in my daughter's best interest.

I was also stuck with the court appointed attorney, her efforts were half hearted. No referrals for services where ever made, no police record produced to verify a history of alcohol abuse or other violations and anyone that wanted to testify against me were allowed, no one that could testify in my behalf, my mom stayed home from work hoping she could testify and the attorney would never called her.

Mom was never allowed to testify about what had been going on. My notes from the paperwork was brushed off she had already decided what she wanted and it wasn't for me to have my family. I was allowed only two character witnesses and that was all.

Regardless that no charges were ever filed, no full investigation done, no background checks no trial by jury. It was a kangaroo court of epic portions.

It would be a whole month before the paperwork of judgments arrived. The judge had ordered my parental rights removed. I immediately pressed my attorney for an attempt to appeal the order, she sat on it. In the last week of the appeal window she mailed the appeal application to my mom's house, were I was staying. The day before annual training 1988 I would receive the package. If I wanted to appeal I had only two days to get the application in, I would have to go AWOL to prove my love for my children.

In the US Code civil action cannot be processed during any period of active duty military service, annual training is by every definition of the law a period of active duty, weekend drills are considered inactive training dates. When I got back from annual training my attorney threw me out of her office and took the appeal application from me stating; **"This is not yours."**

I had completely lost everything and I wouldn't even be

IN THE WORST INTEREST

allowed to say good bye to my girls. The social worker declared that he; "**Didn't care about the wishes of a father, you're not allowed a good bye session and don't need one. Everything will be done to make sure your precious girls will never want to see you, or even speak of you for the rest of their life. You're not worth the effort**"

I had gone to the State Attorney's Office looking to file a complaint, looking for help; instead I was met by an individual who stated: "**Yes, you are right the county has broken the law. You need to consider your children as kidnapped and since you obviously cannot afford the ransom it would be better for society that you forget that they ever existed.**" I would be escorted out off the capital grounds after being found crying heavily on a bench outside of the State Attorney's Office.

The Board of Social Workers didn't require county social workers to carry a license, nor did they have any control over the counties. I would not be allowed to file a complaint the board was completely out of the realm of any policing the profession.

I had nowhere to go, no one would help, and I was abandoned by society itself, not even considered a citizen in the land I was born in, an outcast. I was also thrown out of my family like yesterdays trash and never allowed a final visit the social workers last telephone conservation was "**Only mothers are entitled to a final visit, besides I judge you as a threat to your kids and you don't need to see them. You should of gave up like I was telling you to do, but you're the one to bring on this worthless fight and lost. So sad too bad you're getting what you deserve.**"

LIVING A LIFE WITHOUT MY DAUGHTERS.

MEETING KIM

By now I had been working for a temporary employment service, my primary duties where as a van driver that took the employees to the different job sites throughout the Twin Cities. I knew the areas well and learn the traffic patterns which help in my duties. I also became a problem solver, such there where many job site that I went too where a problem had developed long after the last office worker left for the day.

I got along well with the other employees; it was refreshing that I could be depended on with the other turmoil I had been facing. I was missing my daughters terribly and not being allowed to see them was causing a deep hurt. I had been living with Nick and her boy friend, it was away that kept the bond between us strong and kept me close to work. But I was also getting uncomfortable, I did have feelings for her, luckily the friendship was very strong and it had endured for a lifetime. I needed to move on though.

By the end of September Kim and I started dating. She actually knew Nick from a time when they had worked together at a restaurant in the Riverside district of Minneapolis. It was a good mix, but there was something familiar about each other.

From some reason she said; **"I know not to get in a fight with you."** She was staying at a friend's house, who was sexually exploiting her.

As our dating begun, she planned an escape from his reach. The fellow confront her at work one afternoon and threaten her with a knife, I was on my way to tackle the bum when she bit a chunk out of his arm making him drop the knife. Since it was act work a police report was made and he was barred from the property. We got our own place.

We went to another friend's apartment to lay low and gather our thoughts and make a plan to protect her. Within two weeks we were in our own place south Minneapolis. While there orders for 91C (Army Practical Nurse) Course was submitted and approved.

I would be spending 1989 in San Antonio, Texas. The army was paying St. Philips Community College to allow National Guard and Reserve medics to take the Vocational Nursing Course. It was a year long. Matter of fact the county knew that this was coming and as well denounced it as another reason I needed to lose my parental rights; I had no rights to move my daughters out of the state if they were to grant my parental rights, according to the county.

By the time I met Kim she had given up both of her boys. She had been fighting alcoholism and as she seeking treatment another county social services pressured her in giving her boys up for adoption. Her youngest was to be an open adoption in which she had weekend visits.

As I prepared for the next year school in Texas, mom gave me the book "How to Speak Minnesotan" as a Christmas present. Mom and Kim got along very well it was great to see mom and Kim interact far better than what had happened with my soon to be ex-wife.

Still we all were suffering over lost of the girls.

Robby and I got along great even though it took a little time to get use to me. Others before had abused all of them horribly and as Kim and I would play and interact he often thought I was hurting her, he never heard her laugh so much and was confused.

Still each weekend was better than the last we were bonding together, but my departure was coming up fast. The night before leaving I could not sleep, excited for what changes were ahead, to get beyond what was just endured. Although Kim had a tubal ligation I got her pregnant, news of the pregnant would reach me in San Antonio, she would be coming down around the first of February, she had gotten tired of Minneapolis and wanted to be together.

Prior to Thanksgiving 1988 Kim was given the news that her oldest son was killed and we were given a time and place for the funeral. When we got to the funeral home it turned out to be a cruel joke done by the county social worker that forced her to give her boys up, later we would find out that Jimmy's adopted parent were involve as well.

The county I was dealing with made the notion that they do not recognize the Soldiers and Sailors Civil relief act and made threat that they can summons me from school even if it was military active duty. In the social services opinion the divorce had to be completed before I could go to Texas. I had to do my own paperwork, and then the county sat on the case for nearly a year.

As we prepared for my year of active duty, Kim had made arrangements with her friend to have Robbie over the Easter school break; we got a very nice fully furnished apartment off of Broadway Avenue and close to Fort Sam Houston I could walk to any where I needed to go. Unfortunately an ice storm hit as she arrived and she slipped and fell causing her to miscarry twins.

Although we where estranged from our previous spouses the divorces were not completed. I had left paperwork behind in Minnesota that were to finalize the divorce, but that would not happen for another 9 months.

I would be accused twice by my soon to be ex and her lawyer of fraud; claiming I was falsely taking family pay. I still do not know how these allegations came to be. I was drawing basic allowance for sustenance since we were require due to our class hours and the fact we were not on post for school, we would have to be paying for our meals.

The second time I was accused I was drawn into an army investigation that almost had me kicked out of the school before someone noticed that the allegation was what was false.

I had during this time set up mental health appointments to help get through the pain of being separated from my children. The worker there didn't accept my story and claimed I was hiding something, but don't worry she'll find it out of me. I went there for a while then gave up, nothing was really there for me, it still too much about "The Policy" than being there to help guide fathers through, I has getting what I deserved.

Overall I was doing well in school and I aced the mental health portion, it was joked I must of took notes of what my ex-wife put me through. Yet much of the question on the test started making sense. What had happen and what was needed was far different than what county or I did.

My first wife had a schizophrenic episode, how they usually become known. A violent attack because of the confusion the disease creates in its victims.

Everything I and the county were doing fed into her confusion. The county used the confusion to milk the allegations out of her as a means to create the adoption. My actions just confused her and were seen as a threat. I had more to learn.

By Easter Kim's plans to have Robbie with us were spoiled, by county social services. They chosen not to honor the open adoption and interfered with a claim that we were a threat to him and they would not allow the open adoption to remain. We would never see him until adulthood. He resurfaced recently and was doing very well for himself.

By late spring Kim's daughters would try to run away from their father. They were of mixed race; her family didn't support Kim or the pregnancy and had forced her to surrender her rights to the father. Now that they were teenagers their father had forced them into the sex trade. They were running for their life. Kim's family didn't acknowledge them.

They had called her from a cousin's house and before we could help them they returned home to recover something they left behind. He caught them then executed them at a rest area outside of Kansas City, Missouri. Kim was heartbroken, I was crushed. He got four years for manslaughter for the cold hearted killing of his daughters.

We never got to know where they were buried.

Nursing school continued on, by October Kim's divorce from her first husband, who was serving 5 years for auto theft and drug charges, went through. We were still waiting for mine divorce papers to show up. I would go through the second accusation of falsely drawing family pay, first then a week later my divorce papers finally showed up. I had been divorced for nearly a full month.

We had jokingly said what if we could be married before Halloween. It turned out Halloween would become our wedding day, still the honeymoon would wait. After the ceremony I changed out of my dress "A"'s and got into my uniform for school and back to class I went. By Christmas 1989 I completed the Vocational Nursing Course and returned home to Minnesota and for a renewed life.

One of the sad things to note of this period of time is that had my parental rights had been honored my daughters and I would have had a year of counseling services available for us through the army. Anything that we needed was there, child care, healthcare, and the chance to rebuild, with no addition cost to the tax payer.

Months before completing nursing school Kim heard from her friend Donna. Donnas' husband was in the Army Reserve and had switched to active duty. He was having some problems that he didn't talk to anyone about and one day after coming home from work he smothered their son and left his remains laying in the crib as he popped open a beer.

The county involved in Louisiana acquitted Donna of

any wrong doing, however back in Minnesota county social services stepped in and gave the surviving daughter to the father's mother and interfered with any relationship Donna was to have with her. Claiming not to support or agree with the Louisiana county findings. She had to be involved somehow.

Donnas' ex-husband would spend nearly 5 years in prison before going home and being with his mother and daughter. County social services threaten Donna that if she complained she would never see her daughter again. She was secretly seeing her daughter through the grandmother.

We stayed up all night before the flight home. Kim never flew before so she was very nervous and scared. She slept like a rock all the way home. Nick met us at the airport and went to my mom's house to start job hunting and search for our own place. We found a small apartment, I tried to see if I could get back on the fire department but the changes from my high school years and the current leadership was very disappointing. I would be better off moving somewhere else and try there than to stay in my home town.

I had also contacted my social worker for two reasons; one to see if he had a change of heart and would let me have a final visit with my daughters, the second was for post adoption services. Mainly a file as required by law that would had allowed me to send letters and gifts to. He gave neither, just stated that I was **"A failure to adjust."** Then he hung up the telephone on me.

I went to work at a hospital as I waiting for the date of my nursing exam. I would be working on the orthopedic ward. Though it was good work as I prepared for the night shift the nurse I was to work with threw a fit that she did not what to work with any nurse with a temporary license and waiting for board. The hospital used my termination the previous ambulance service as a means to justify sending me on my way. Then they failed to send me my final check. I had to sue for it.

In March 1990 a unit from the National Guard was going to South Korea for a training game called Team Spirit. A medic had been released from the Guard for being charged with domestic violence and child abuse and they needed a replacement quick. I had five days to get my things in order and go in his place.

Our flight took off in the early morning hours after spending the night at the West Saint Paul Armory. We had a stop in Anchorage Alaska and Tokyo, Japan. As we were landing our 747 was struck by lightning, the lights flickered off then back on. We would spend some extra time on the ground as the plane was checked over there was the threat that we may have to spend the night however the plane took off and we got to Korea later in the day, we would have a long bus ride to our camp where the tents and vehicles waited for us.

South Korea was a beautiful place, the mountains, the fields and the cities and towns in between had such an appeal. However we arrived to our camp at evening twilight three of us slept in the ambulance for the first night. We wouldn't see our camp until day bright. The army HMMWV Ambulance does not have windows in the passenger compartment like the old Dodge ambulances had. So when the back doors were opened we were blinded by the break sunlight. Our camp was in a river bed with farm fields behind us and a road on the bank across the stream from us.

Nearby was a small town where we could go, though rarely, to the public shower to clean up and have a nice hot shower. Since most homes in South Korea didn't have running water it was these public showers that the local citizens would use a couple times a week to stay clean, everything else was as if I was on the family farm right before grandpa died.

Much of what we did was take care of the medical needs of the soldiers and hung out. Most of the training was focused on paper drills that didn't require much that the motion of the work it takes to run gun lines in a warzone, no artillery shots were ever fired but the movement was done as if they were. After the first week I was moved to a line company after the river had risen and flooded the camp do to a night of rain.

The next week was in constant movement every day the gun

line company would move from one firing position to another. The guns were set up and the camouflage set up over the gun. But as like with all the other placements we never fired a shot, just went through the movement, including setting up the survey stake that is used to help aim the gun.

Somewhere in here I remember taking a soldier to the hospital, I really cannot remember why just that we ended up at the clinic that traces its lineage to the very 5077th MASH that the TV show was loosely based from.

From there we ended up in the battalion trains areas the units pulled together for the final movement to Camp Page and to clean and prep our equipment to return home, three weeks was spent there. I did get one time to go to town during the training. Most of us were hoping for a chance to see the DMZ, but issues between North and South Korea stopped the trip from happening.   •

On our R&R day our driver got lost and we almost made it the border before we turned around, we were in civilian clothes and I was without a jacket. I was frozen by the time we reached town, so the first thing was get a jacket to stay warm. That was most of my money. So I spent most of my time wandering the town.

Once at the base we spent four days cleaning and packing equipment and gear. This was mid March and the weather switched between nice and miserable, just waits 15 minutes and you could have your pick to what type of climate you wanted.

The day on the wash rack we had to clean every speck of dirt off the trucks, I washed Wisconsin clay from Fort McCoy off the trucks in Korea, from places on the truck you never knew would had ever existed. It was well after sunset when we were done with the last truck, the next day was the flight home.

In 1990 I had participated in 5 annual training periods and would do the same in 1991, matter of fact it wasn't uncommon to do three or more annual training periods each year throughout my career in the Army National Guard. The work for the most part was consistent, it kept our bills pay. And during the period I was waiting for the nursing board kept me busy.

On the day of the Nursing Board I found that the National Registry Exam for Emergency Medical Technician far more difficult and challenging, but I would have to wait a month before I got my results, until then it was back to temporary employment to keep the apartment paid for and food on the table.

The State Lottery started in 1990 on the day I got word that I had passed the Nursing board I had won a $50.00 scratch off. Kim and I went out to celebrate. My first job as a LPN was with a pediatric home nursing service. I was providing nursing care to medical risk children in their homes.

In the midway area I was working with one 2 year old girl who her sister and her had developed a serious lung ailment as their family escaped Laos and Cambodia and the refugee camp that they stayed until the U.S. brought them over.

Her sister was so serious that she remained in the care of the county social services, while she got to stay home and try to have as normal of a life as possible. She had spent so much time with an IV in her foot she never got to learn how to walk; she got around on her butt.

Since the girls relied so heavily on county services the father was never allowed to work by county social services. Being of a tribal culture this was very hard on the family. Mom and Dad would get into arguments, mainly because Dad wanted to work. Some of my fellow nurses plotted to dismantle the family, for the moms and children sake. I couldn't support the efforts. I had a better relationship with the family.

A bill came up in the Minnesota Legislation that was to give the county social workers unprecedented powers and no adequate check and balance. I talked to my employer before planning any lobbing to fight it. Instead I was asked to leave my job; my past experience with county social services had created a conflict with my employer. I would discover I had a grim choice, fight for father's rights, no work. Work and forget about father rights. The pain of not having my daughters was overbearing.

Off and on I would lobby to change the thing that I went through, most to attentive ears, and shocked looks when the paperwork would be torn through, still no answer on how to get me reconnected with my daughters. The system was better prepared to take apart families that to put families together.

By now I was preparing to join another local volunteer fire department. For the time being I was back in the life I knew so well. I had taken a job at a nursing home close by. I had also started another job at a home health group that had me working in the medical needs foster home of same county social services that took my parental rights away.

In the foster home it met a boy that would tear my heart out. He was that child who should have been in my daughters' bed. The same county social worker so bent on removing my rights so that my daughters could be given up for adoption. He sent the boy home for the eighth time to be beaten into a coma by his mother. Now he lay in a bed, arms and legs tightly tractured muscle antropied needing hourly exercising and tube feedings, the boy was a body that simply breathed and that was all this child would do for the rest of his life.

He was in such a deep vegetative state that to say what was actually alive was impossible to tell. All we knew was that only a single layer of living brain cells where what lined his brain, everything else was gone. Nights were mainly spent between his cares and the family's laundry.

The household were mostly girls and since they were all over 16 I had basketful of sexy nightgowns waiting to be washed.

What hurt the most was here was the child that truly needed the beds my daughters were taking. All for a mother's revenge this child had truly suffered his mom for hating the fact she had him, my daughters were simply to be used as an expression of their mothers anger against a father. For angers sake three children suffered in their own ways, one was totally maimed.

How much more did this really cost. Monetarily it was in

the millions if not in the billions. But for this one young boy it was his life that was paid the highest price, and all for simple revenge a mother was forced eight times to care for a child she didn't even want alive.

Kim met up with an old friend Karen, who had two boys Robyn and Nate. Karen had just been released from county jail for the rape of several boys in an inner city apartment complex, she had served 11 months with a six month probation in which she was allowed full unsupervised custody of her two sons each weekend.

She was on a heavy dose of anti-depressants and other psychotropic medications which were conflicting with the pain killers her mental health doctor was prescribing. Matter of fact the amount of pills she was taking fill two large grocery bags to over flowing and signs of the adverse reactions when all around.

During the weekend visits Kim and I were noticing some disturbing trends; the youngest was acting out heavily and very violently. The oldest was withdrawn, they both stated they felt safest around Kim and myself and were asking if they could stay with us. Kim and I thought very hard and talk through what we were seeing and hearing from the boys, so in late spring we moved Karen and her boys in with us.

Not knowing what would happen next, just that the thought that county social services did not require parenting classes or to check the home for sexual abuse after Karen had pleaded guilty for raping young boys in a Minneapolis apartment complex.

We knew if anything we could help Karen bridge into a more successful family life if there was someone that to guide her there. We were surprise what we discovered next.

We went in on a three bedroom manufactured home, but shortly after moving in Kim discovered Karen molesting her boys and the work of documenting and turning her over to the police begun. I was working both at the same temporary agency that I met Kim at and at an Urgent Care in the north metro, but would lose the later job when I ran into difficulties in communicating with county social services.

Only help we really got was through a very caring social worker who went far out of her way for all of us.

Instead we had to sneak the boys out of the home. Nick help by allowing the oldest boy a chance to stay overnight with her and her husband. We all met at the police station in the morning. The detective had built a thick report from what Kim and the boys had presented. Since much of the abuse occurred while I was at annual training Kim had documented the abuse in letters she was writing me. We had to explain to Karen what was going on and that we were trying to get her the help she needed. The police came and arrested her for the abuse and the boys went to foster care for a few nights, then they got their wish to stay with us.

The fall school year was one of great challenges, early morning counseling sessions and meetings with the county had us often dropping Nate, the youngest, at school an hour early were he would go read a book at the school library. He was doing much better, no longer acting out in violence he had been interacting with his classmates very well. The oldest was having his issues as well. The stability that Kim and I created he was thriving on.

Robyn, the oldest, was constantly asking me about having my permission to bring his girl friend over for sex. Kim having a better understanding about the difficulties for teenage sex abuse victims had than I did, however at 14 I didn't feel that it was my permission that he truly needed. He needed to develop the sense of self discipline that allowed him to make the safest and best decision for himself.

I wouldn't give into the pressure both he and Kim were putting me through. This only deepens the conflict between all of us.

I did however make sure he had condoms to encourage that if he did make his decision that it would be the safe decision. October had me in Panama for the National Guard. I was on a three week KPUP Mission where National Guard and reserve soldiers would spend some time with active duty units training and working in their military specialties. I would spend my first four days in the jungle helping with the Expert Field Medical Badge Testing since I held the badge myself since 1983 while I was in Germany.

The next two weeks I would work in the battalion aid station of an aviation support battalion (Blackhawk helicopter) at Fort Kolbe. I would spend my weekends with the rest of my group at Fort Clayton. On our off time we spent some on Taboga Island on the Pacific Ocean side. At Fort Clayton we had a front seat view of the canal and large ships would pass through all day long.

One in our group had decided to stay on for one final week and the rest of us went home. The trip home was far less eventful than going there. While at the Miami Airport on the way to Panama our group was approached by a small group of prostitutes has we hurried to catch our flight, nothing like that on the return, or maybe we were to tried to notice but it was great to be home. Within a week the 1991 Halloween Blizzard would occur.

My car had lost its engine just the day before and was now towed away to the junk pile. The driver's door didn't work and there was a hole in the floor by the passenger's seat. I often got in the car through the back door and jumped over the seat to get to the fire station and work. The beating that the fire calls caused was just too much and it finally gave out.

Nick had given me her mountain bike until we could get a car from Kim's lifelong friend Helen. However we had to put up with the three day effect of the blizzard before we could get down to Rosemount and get it.

The morning of November 1st 1991 I awoke to the banshee cry of tones, a fire alarm was sounding and I needed to get to the fire station. I first had to push the door open. Even though I had shoveled snow several times during the night I was met by waist deep snow as I grasped the bike and begun pedaled the two and a half miles to the fire station. I had gotten into a rhythm that had me doing flying dismount as I hurdle the bicycle over the windrows of the snowplows trying to clear the street of the near 24 inches of snow. I arrived to the fire station 20 minutes after the tones, to be only the fourth person arrive there. Two went out on the truck, the only ones that made it by car, Mike made it on cross country skis and I on the bicycle.

We would spend the next 24 hours in the fire station to facilitate emergency response since the snow was so deep and the fact it took over two days to dig the cities out enough to go home. Later we would go get the car from Helen and I was back on the road. By now I had a new nursing job with a nursing pool. One of the places I would work at was a medical needs group home.

One of Kim's friends worked there. If I had stayed a pool nurse I may had done very well. However the need of health insurance I gave it a go to try to work there fulltime. Up to then the nursing pool environment was working; it gave me variety and just enough stress to keep me functional. I was thriving, the fire calls and training, guard drills and work was almost to near harmony.

I had talked my guard unit to sponsor a Boy Scout Explorer Post were we took young adults and with extensive first aid training went and provided first aid stations for scouting and civic events. Things truly were looking up.

It wasn't a very large post but it worked very well and the eight girls and one boy had their hearts in a great place. I had passed on the torch that Chief McLean gave me.

The kids were doing great. Maybe at the meetings they were a little too energized from the week of school and friends, but whenever we did an event they knew the job well. Into the second year I tried two things to help make the program better. The first was to establish First Responder Training for these young adults; I would spend a year and a half working the issue.

I worked very hard for the success of the explorer program.

I had issued a letter writing campaign to ask for donations. I was trying to raise $3,000.00 to add civilian equipment to the pool of military equipment that I drew to training the kids with. Federal law allows for some military assistance with scouting program for this purpose. Of the 1000 letters I wrote and sent, only two were answered. One was for a $500.00 check; the other was **"Although your program sounds very interesting and beneficial for young adult. It is not in out interest to support programs like yours."** The signee was a business that shares sponsorship of the Metrodome Scoreboard, the other sponsor never returned a reply to their letter.

Still the program worked well. Robyn himself was doing well with the program, but the holidays were coming and a bigger problem was looming. Karen was blocking the only funds we were allowed to help take care of her boys, we got no assistance from county social services other than a very understanding Child Protection Worker. She was very aware of the previous case with county social services. We were doing everything right and the boys were doing better than what they did while in foster care.

It was hands down I got the chance I wanted with my daughters through these boys. With all the problems it was working very well for everyone. Some of the problems were by the very support services that county social services used in their Child Protection Department cases.

A conflict of interest with one was very apparent when Robbie and Leanne showed up at the clinic, we had stumbled into the clinician who interfered with Kim's open adoption agreement, as well as the one who did the adoption counseling for my daughters, we felt that an unhealthy arrangement had been made and our social worker agreed so another mental health worked was found.

Everything was working well, almost too well. With the holidays coming Robyn got his hopes way too high. We were bonding very well but the amount of depression he suffered Christmas 1991 threw me for a loop. Right after the New Years

1992 he started making a very distinct homicide and suicide plan, he needed help. More help than I could give him for that moment. I put him into inpatient therapy.

County social services got mad. Our social worker broke us the news the county was pulling the boys and placing them into the foster home system. Part of the depression came from the fact Karen had died in custody for an anxiety induced asthma attack when she missed shower time. No one in her family, or the boy's father would take them. We weren't allowed because my decision to place Robyn in the hospital for his needs and the embarrassment that **"I created for county social services."**

Our social worker told us that she was thankful that we went farther than what any of their paid foster parents would had done, and we were never paid to be there or to care for them. We just did the best we could do and better than anyone thought we would had done.

The supervisor of county child protection at the time had a different take. His views came in a heated telephone call; **"What the $%^& to you think embarrassing us this way."** He shouted in the phone at me. **"You made us take your girls away from you. If you had shown us the kind of judgment that you have shown with these boys you would still have your daughters today."** My comeback was simple; **"All county social services saw was blond hair and blue eyes and great disposition. They were adoptable. No one cared what I was capable of as a parent or even what the law required. My wife and the original social worker sole focused were to get my rights removed for the adoption."** His final comment was **"We are never worried about birth fathers. Besides the needs of the child supersede the requirement of the law and if we determine that it is in the child best interest to break the law then so be it. It is not like you will amount to anything anyways and who cares if we break the law anyway for some pitiful mans kids, birthparents really don't count to us anyways."**

The boys were now gone. Emotionally it had a negative effect.

I was having behavior problems at the fire department and I was bouncing from job to job, mainly because I was working 4 to 5 different jobs trying to meet the bills and the cost of day living. Months later I would make a very bad mistake.

During Christmas Time the fire department would do Santa Claus tours of the communities. It was fun to dress up, funny thing was the fire fighters would stop at their homes for their kids, but when Nate and Robyn were with us they would not take the time to stop at my house, like at the other fire fighters homes. A hostile work environment had been developing and growing.

Many of the rookie class I was in were having problems. One of our fire fighters had committed suicide with implications of a sexual involvement with the fire chief. I had helped another fire fighter set up a fire fighter explorer post with the fire department as well, and I took them to the Boy Scouts Ripley Rendezvous at Camp Ripley, Minnesota where we assisted with first aid services.

But the relationship between the fire chief and my wife was very hostile. She wasn't allowed in the station, though she didn't drive and had medical needs the fire chief's opinion of women were expressed as trollops and bimbos that men were better off without.

One fire fighter would later on confine in me of sexual advances he took from the chief. The Department of Human Rights was there to protect others from Caucasians men; the quote was **"We are not going to waste our money when we know who the problems are."** The familiar pattern was returning again, Bret was having problems dealing with it.

THEN I MAKE A STUPID MISTAKE.

Emotionally I was holding up but not as well as I thought. The fire department that I was on had a very hostile working environment with male on male sexual harassment, hazing and I was buckling under my own demons. So many times when we tried to leave the station the heavy traffic on the highway was difficult to enter, I had gotten edgy with the near misses of accidents that we were witnessing to get out of the station and flipped a car off as I pulled my fire jacket on. I got a 5 day suspension for that.

I was heavy hearted to begin with from calling attorneys through the St. Paul telephone book and getting the same answer. I called on who was once a state representative from the south metro area that I grew up in. I was alone trying to deal with the effects of my children being removed from my life.

I knew this attorney from the days of my father, while alive he had been a lobbyist for the Machinist Union. He had been to my dad's funeral along with so many other elected officials from every level of government. I was floored when I was told; **"An attorney's breakfast has to come before a poor man's justice."** Many pains were tearing through me, I could simply work away the time and have money, a house, and all the other material niceties of life or keep trying to find away to have my children in my life, just not both.

Two problems were forming; both the co-ed guard unit I was in and the work places were caring heavy sexual overtones between employees. I found myself with all the emotional damage of the previous year's hanging on the ledge of a sexual affair. Many hints would be repelled, but still my values and self discipline had been undermined. I needed to relearn almost like an emotional rehab was needed, everything was turned upside down.

I was still working at the group home and would for almost two years, I spilt my night shift between two different facilities that the service ran. At the one home a became friends with co-worker. She was young and just out of high school and we got along very well, I got along with much of the staff. She stood out, we got way too close.

She hit a nerve, a release from the emotional baggage that had been piling up. Kim was having too many difficulties with the fire department, the explorer post, and the thing her father put her through and we had been fighting way too much, she still loved me and I loved her, just didn't like the things I did afraid that I was trying to get myself killed.

At work she gave a peace that I had never had before. It took almost six months but the friendship slowly turned sexual, with us sneaking time with each other. Like Kim she didn't drive so I would pick her up and take home from work, that's where we found the opportunities. It would last for nearly four months before we found a way to end it and try to return to our normal lives.

We were both at fault, we had both filled a void that our partners were missing and found that we had undermined the respect and commitment we made to others. We had hurt the trust of others in our lives. Now we both had to rebuild our value base and repair the damage the affair had caused.

I often see this moment as an awaking of the broken spirit

that was caused by the divorce from my first wife and the emotional abuse from county social services.

The kids I had worked on were victims of serious abuse and birth defects. The affair caused a strain at work and I was force to leave. Later on I heard of rumors that she was pregnant. We had discussed this issue when we split, I would have to wait until the child turned 18 before I would ever be allowed to see it. We went back to our lives as if it never happened, never talking to each other again.

For the explorer post I was working with the State Department of Health to gain full approval to train the 14 plus kids to the level of First Responder.

At one of the Camporee were we provided first aid services I was approached by another adult leader from another scout unit that took me aside, he was the cop who handcuffed me the day of the big fight in September 1985.

He had asked what the outcome to the case was and broke into to tears when I told him that I had lost my parental rights. We talked about the policy and how everything that appeared wrong, the two stories didn't match, the scene didn't match the story told at the police station. Policy didn't allow for question to be asked. I should have never lost my rights in the first place. Nothing the police found would had justified it.

The neighbor that had backed up my first wife's allegation had never step foot in our apartment and had a lengthy history of mental health issues herself and the police knew not to rely on her comments, but the county social services had their own ideas and their own ways of doing things.

It would take nearly a full year to get the approval of the state for the First Responder training for the scouts; the only problem was the National Guard shut the program down the day before the approval was given, again another crushing blow and I felt betrayed.

My unit had been preparing to go to Guatemala for a support mission, I was ready to go. However after these two events I needed to stay home and collect my thoughts, I was really feeling hurt and didn't feel up to the trip emotionally.

I had been doing 3 to 5 annual training periods a year since returning to Minnesota from California, collecting military retirement points along the way. I felt very empty with the explorer post gone.

I started working for a school bus company to keep health insurance on Kim and she was working as a bus aid. During the school year with the multiple checks we started to gain on our bills. Summers became the drag when not enough work could be found.

1994 A YEAR OF
DRAMATIC CHANGES

During the demises of the affair we gave up the trailer and rented an apartment nearby. I was now a third of the distance from the fire station and was often able to catch the first truck out the door.

The fire department had built several new fire stations and we welcomed the addition of several new trucks, including a 110 foot ladder truck that required a tiller driver to help steer the near 50 foot long truck. It was fun driving the back end of the truck.

By spring a problem developed, turned out our landlord was pocketing money and even though I always asked Kim to make sure she got receipts there were several months were receipts were not received for the rent paid. We were given an eviction notice.

As we were packing to move a fire broke out in the other building of our complex. Smoke was bellowing into a third floor apartment, but where was the fire? My first assignment was to open a hallway wall in the stairwell. I stayed professional rather than personal and made the opening to the size needed. We had a cool wisp of smoke but no heat, no flames.

Continuing our search we find a crawl space under the stairwell, since I am rather a small size at 5'7" and only weigh at the time at 155 lbs I easily entered the space and found the source of the smoke, it was in fact a fire. The building was over 30 years old and the front stairs had separated from the building. Smokers had been using the crack between the stairs and the building as an ashtray and by now a pile of cigarette butts layer almost a foot thick and it was smoldering.

While at that apartment complex we met Kay and her kids Jenna, Josh, Tasha and later Larissa. Jenna was more the parent than her mother and Jenna was the age of my oldest daughter. There was a strong connection and for a while I could feel my daughter's presence within her. Kay's kids spent a lot of time at our apartment, we became their safe house when it was needed.

There were a group of families that Kay knew that would spend the weekend with card games and drinking. Kay herself didn't drink, just help keep the games going and socialize. All these families' kids though ended up in our apartment. The kids didn't want to be around all the drinking and smoking. We had games and a quiet place to catch some sleep while the party at their apartment continued through the night.

Kim and I moved to an apartment near to the trailer park we had left only year prior.

There we met Lynn and her two daughters Penny and Sammy. Penny was a loud and over bearing 14 year old that started spreading rumors that she and I were having an affair. Bragging how great of the sex we were having. I became livid with the pain her actions were causing both Kim and I. I was more ill to this runaway imagination. To the point we had to involve the police.

Still the kids that adopted Kim and I as an Aunt and Uncle were visiting us on a regular basis. By now nearly each weekend was a different group of kids spending the night at our apartment.

On the Guard side a sexual affair in a Military Police unit

made the local news, policies were being developed that curb the trend and the damage. The age difference between the male and female genders of this situation was over 20 years and other problems had formed around it. It was more a sexual assault than an affair, or was it?? All I know that from that point on us leaders in the National Guard were under orders to stop the sexual fraternization across the ranks. If it looked wrong we were to get involved.

The beginning of 1994 an arson spree had hit the cities. Striking commercial properties the group had a shopping list and a team approach to their theft. Getaway cars would park near the rear emergency exits while two teams entered the target. Each team would split between the tasks of setting up the steal, there was those how grasped the targeted items, those who pour accelerant and the igniter.

In a series of very quick movements the store would have multiple fires lit in the store the teams would then race to the nearest fire exit with merchandise in hand to the getaway car. They had set up a very pronounced pattern that was easy to watch, more importantly it appeared they were heading into the jurisdiction of my fire department; we were briefed on what to expect.

By late spring their first fire in our area would hit a business in a nearby community then one in another. By mid July they would hit a business in our jurisdiction. It would be a long night, over four hours we worked on the fire. There would be a public fire education event for the day; we would have minimal sleep before conducting the event on a beautiful Sunday.

I was in my fire fighters uniform and ushering at church when the pagers went off for another fire call. I left the church to report to the station afterward four of us would take the ladder truck to public display in a park.

We mainly made sure no one did anything that could get them hurt on the truck. We took turns climbing the 110 foot ladder and took pictures of the Minneapolis skyline that was visible from the top. At one point I left to use the bathroom.

I never made it to the bathroom, having stopped and talked to another explorer post that I was trying to set up some joint meeting opportunities for the kids. When I got back to the truck I found something very alarming.

There were a group of three girls the youngest was 13 and the oldest was 17 making sexual commits to the fire fighters. They were grabbing at them and making sexual jokes of how great they would be if the guys would have sex with them. These girls were a part of the group who were performing there.

Before I could fully react the guys dumped the girls on me and began to coax them into harassing me. Joe one of the younger fire fighters stated **"What's a matter? Can't handle a bunch of girls?"** And things got worst from there. The fire fighter in charge had forbidden me from contacting the scout leader of the girls and then the girls started getting physical, grabbing at me and attempted to fondle my butt.

At one time the youngest girl in the group had grabbed me hard on the butt and whispered in my ear **"And, I'll give you better sex than your wife would ever dream to."** I had attempted to walk away but the girls grasped my arms at try to pull me behind the truck. I took off into a run; nothing else was left to try.

The following Monday I was asked to resign from the fire department and turn in my gear. As I turned in my gear the fire chief struck my wife who had accompanied me. We left the station. I had lost trust in the system and knew I couldn't make a police complaint, for it would never be investigated. The city attorney wasn't any help either, it was better to cover everything up.

The fellow fire fighter who had confided to me about the chief sexual behaviors, finally found the strength to report the sexual misconduct of the fire chief to the state. But again no one would take our complaints. The Department of Human Rights would not get in between a disagreement with a fire chief and his fire fighters. The fire chief on the other hand would leave the department months before he could gain the longest standing fire chief in state history.

He would die two months after retirement. The new fire chief didn't do any of us any favors and we were left abandoned by the agency that pitifully abused us.

We both became fire fighters for the drive within us to serve our communities, for both of us it was taken away. I don't know what was worst enduring what Penny had been doing to Kim and I almost daily or the fact that the 13 year old was the group leaders' daughter. All I wanted was a letter of apology. What I got was indifference everyone denied their part of the situation and I was left out in the cold and out of the service I enjoy giving to my community.

I was forced to resign if I was to have any chance to keep a career in fire fighting. But I would have to move away from Minnesota if I was to have any fire fighting career at all, no department in Minnesota would dishonor a fire chief.

However in August of 1994 large forest fires were burning across the western states and the manpower for fighting the fires were growing thin. Just weeks after the 14 were killed on the Storm Mountain Fire I answered a plea from the Minnesota Department of Natural Resources for fire fighters to go out west.

After passing the agility test 400+ individuals were sent to Grand Rapids, Minnesota for Forest Fire Fighter training. I brought my training records with me and added them to the training file that was produced for this incident. Since there was a shortage of Squad Bosses my fire fighting and military history made me eligible to become one on my rookie forest fire. I would also take the role of crew medic for a 20 man hand crew.

After the training was completed we were loaded in a plane and sent to Kalispell, Montana. It would be a long night bus ride to the furthest northwest corner of the state. Our camp would be only 13 miles from the Canadian and Idaho border.

We would arrive at 5 am and would be allowed about 4 hours of sleep before being placed on the line.

Since the camp was wakening for a day on the number of fires that made up the Yaak Red Dragon Complex we were to sleep on the slope of a mountain. While one fire fighter grabbed the box that held sleeping pads I grabbed the box that held paper sleeping bags, which were used to help guard the frosty morning air, to sleep in.

We mostly just slid down the hill.

When we got up we had breakfast and were handed a bag lunch and loaded into a bus to be dropped off and start the climb to the fire. The drop point was at an intersection of the main and subordinate logging road that help create a clear cut area that we hiked through. The climb was 1000' to the ridge and were the fire was stopped by the gallant efforts of a hand crew that the following day were going back home to Wisconsin.

Our crew was a mixed of individuals from nearly 20 states that make up the ninth Forest Service Region. Many of us had never seen each other until this incident and now not only had to work together, I was leading 5 of them.

As we set to re-enforce the line of the trail was a heavily burning stump. It was over 300' from the fire break but was something to look out as the day went on. One thing we had did was brought over 3000' of fire hose with use and we were preparing to make it a wet line. First was to get our bearings and assess what we were up against and clean up the hasty line that held overnight and our delay to the fire.

We started to mop up. Putting out the hot spots that were close to the line and working our way to 300' into the area brunt by the fire. One problem we had was with the water delivery. The trucker running the water truck had never done fire work before and was concerned if he let the water flow out of his tank that it would ruin our portable tank that we were pumping from. He didn't carry a pump on the trailer so every time he would put water in the portable tank our pump would be diverted to pump the water out of his truck.

Another problem came on the opposite side of the ridgeline. The drop off point was about 2500' elevation, the ridgeline was 1000' above that on the opposing side of the ridgeline in dropped to below the 2000' elevation. We only needed the pump to start the water flow the weight of the water once below the elevation of the portable tank would siphon out of it. The problem came about 2000' below the ridgeline, our hose line was splitting under the pressure the siphon was causing.

The rest of the water we needed would have to be pump from a lake in the valley below, or buck dropped by helicopter. We would work 6 days on this part of the fire to include one day to recover and airlift the supplies out of the valley. As for the stump that was burning on the first day, after lunch I went to check it out. It had burned out completely without any intervention. As I was inspecting it a snag fell and drop across my path that I had left, reminding me of how dangerous the situation I was in. I rejoined my squad and went back to the fire.

In the valley was a chain of lakes call the Fishy Lakes on the Forest Service maps, the cut throat trout that surface and the nearby hot coals had all of us dreaming of a fish fry lunch, event the fire was named Fish Fry Fire. Still we behaved ourselves and continued working the line. As a crew we worked very well together.

Working with the forest fire crews was one of the best experiences of my life. Gone was the hostile environment that previous fire department held. The Forest Service followed the labor laws closely any infraction was met with the fact that you would be buying you plane ticket home or worst.

During one night a fire fighter was raped in the shower trailer. The suspect was nabbed as the crews returned for the line for the day. Gone were the days that men couldn't be the victim, this place took it very seriously. A post incident briefing was given to inform what had happen and counseling was available. A very big change from what I was used to, I had found a place where I could be comfortably fit in.

We worked very long days on the fire line for three weeks we had worked over 12 hours a day with no day off, got up before sunrise and back to bed after dark. It was a job of adventure, of calling, I had found myself.

We saw many different sides of our assigned fire. Helicopter airlifted supplies out of the fire area when no longer needed, since that was the safer way to carry the equipment rather than to try to carry all the hose, pumps and other supplies across steep slopes and spree fields that make up the scene.

My 20 man crew got trough the fire without a single injury or serious illness. Many crews were not that lucky. Our camp had grown to 4000 fire fighters and support staff; I knew the medical staff well from getting supplies to help keep my crew healthy, moleskin for blisters. The simple rule was once back at camp go to the shortest line whichever it may be; chow, phones, supply, commissary, or showers it didn't matter the order you going to see all of them anyways so to the shortest line you go.

One day working the line I had developed nine blisters on my feet but continued on with the job. I had worn out a pair of combat boots on the line from 6 mile hikes into the fire and sometime walking over 20 miles on the line during the day. Within days we demob and went home.

A couple of memories from this first fire included the chewing gum contest on our bus two of our fire fighters worked to see who could chew the most stick of gum at one time. Back at camp there was a table with treats on it. There were limits on how many packs of gum or bags of chips and candy we could take; no limits for the granola bars and other healthy treats to take on the line. So we all stocked up for the contest and the bus driver stopped short of the camp as the 120th stick of gum was worked into the mouth of the fire fighter and he struggled to chew.

Another memory was had when one evening as we drove out of the northern most access to the fire was to see the return of animals as they watch us drive by. It was like being on a zoo tour bus every turn had another animal, Moose, Deer, Bear both black and Grizzly, even a Mountain Lion watched us as we watched them in amazement, I wish digital camera would had been about a decade earlier such a missed opportunity.

The work was hard and dangerous, but I can work in a dangerous environment doesn't mean I for thrill take reckless risks. Safety has to be the focus even when a large helicopter with a bucket extended on a 120 foot line is hovering over head by inches.

We all shared the mountain valley and I was manning a gated wye as the squad worked in two teams each on their own hot spots and a pump operator below keeping the water flowing. Later in the week we slung all the hose and pumps out of the mountain valley and continued to another part of the fire.

It would take almost six weeks before we would see the pay check and when I got home I was picked up by the bus company from the DNR office and immediately put on a school bus route.

By the time I got to the last school of the day I was running about 45 minutes behind and with a screaming teacher at my door. Blaming me for failing to learn the route before the start of the school year, she yelled wanting my name to turn me in. I pleaded the fact that I just got back from being in Montana, my bags of clothes were on the floor by the door. She looked down and again at my DNR hat when it all connected together.

The next day I would get my route for the year. I was missing the fire pager.

I met up with a local fire fighter from another community who was a part of a volunteer emergency response service that provided for community events. I brought the explorer equipment to them and we developed our own, using the First Responder Program to train them. I also join a local Boy Scout Troop as well. My intentions were to rebuild my leadership skills.

I still did nursing shifts with one at the first nursing home that my first wife was fired from for abusing a resident. While taking report the charge nurse reported **"(name withheld) had called again during the previous evening shift and was harassing the staff."** We were reminded to inform her that she is not to be calling to any telephone be the home or private residents in the facility. I felt a rock in my throat when I asked what the woman's last name was and the head nurse look at me and said **"We need to talk."**

Turned out my first wife had been making these telephone calls since the months leading up to her firing. Four months before our last fight. She had a crush on the resident whom she was calling and threatening the staff if she felt they were not taking good care of him. County social services would never take any complaint from the facility though whenever they reported her actions. She was protected by county social services.

By now this behavior of hers had been going on for nearly 10 years. This would be one of the last times I would work as a nurse. In January of 1995 I change jobs from the school bus company and switched to public para-transit service.

Our health insurance dropped us from insurance as Kim was diagnosis with severe asthma which was being aggravated by the fumes from the buses. We needed health insurance and had many bills pile up during the period that I worked uninsured as a nurse.

In 1995 I approached new fire chief as an act of peace so that if either between the National Guard and the DNR sent me into any of the communities for a disaster assistance assignment there would be no hard feelings. He had leaned back in his chair and reassures that he **"Didn't see any situation that any of the cities would need either DNR or National Guard support."**

KIM GOES BACK TO HIGH SCHOOL

In the spring of 1995 Kim decided to complete the high school diploma that she had dropped from as a means of getting away from problems at home. At the same time I was under review to a documentation error I did back when I worked with the medical group home.

The Board of Nursing would put a condition on my nursing license and even promised that I would be able to keep working as a nurse as I met their requirements for additional training.

First I could not find anyone that would hire a LPN with a conditional license, second I didn't have the money for the classes the nursing board wanted me to take. The National Guard would send me to a military course that would had exceeded their training requirements but the board ruled that the military program as substandard and not appropriate for their needs, however they never looked at any of the training material to make that judgment, it was **"We are not going to waste our time for what we feel about the U.S. Military."**So a stalemate existed in another part of my life.

May 1995 brought a very interesting weekend to mind. I had met up with a group of friends that set up another emergency services explorer post that I used the equipment from the previous post with. The leader of the group was also a promoter of charity professional wrestling matches. He needed volunteer security at the matches so I went along on a couple of them.

At a match for local high school band I posted myself at the door. I had been worked into the script for the day's match; however I am a lousy actor. One spectator though was standing out. He had brought his three children with him the oldest about 16 and the youngest about 12.He encouraged them to entice the wrestlers, to mock them. He stood on the folding chair and shouted making threats and jeers at the wrestlers. The kids just lowered their heads in embarrassment of their fathers' actions. He was the old social worker, the very one that claimed that **"Any father who wrestles with his daughters is most defiantly preparing to sexual abuse them."**

Intermission came; I was standing guard to the right of popular national wrestler as he signed black and white pictures of him and his brother. The social worker dragged his kids to the line even as they protested and begged to go home. He stepped next to me, turning he looked at my name tag and turned white.

He left the line and returned to his seat drawing his knees to his chest and remained in that position for the rest of the match. His kid's stood silent; bewildered they moved with the line and return to their seats as well, again he never moved or even addressed his own kids or even the wrestlers in the ring.

A police officer on duty there was questioning me; did I say anything to him to create this dramatic change in the gentleman's behavior? We had initially talked about the social workers actions prior to intermission and I had briefly explained my history to the officer.

When it was verified that I said nothing to him, not a single word the police officer stated **"Then he is feeling awful guilty about something."** When the match ended the social worker and his family simply disappeared, the whole second half of the match he never moved from his position and not a word was said. No they were all simply gone as if they were never there in the first place.

Another thing I did for the spring was to get an amateur radio license and take SkyWarn training becoming a storm chaser, but I had to get a radio first.

I was also taking Basic Non-Commissioned Officer Course. This required monthly drills at the Minneapolis Veterans Administration Hospital and annual training in Indiana.

During the August guard drill weekend I got called away to assist with the Sag-Corridor Fire in the Boundary Water Canoe Area along the Minnesota and Canadian border. I was assigned to a crew that was on initial attack standby in Ely, Minnesota.

For the first week we mainly painted the forest service center as we watched the air tankers fly over head to the distant smoke columns of the multiple fires that merged into one. Our job was to put out any other fire that broke out, there were a couple and we kept them small. Granted the second fire that broke out three of us where flow to by a forest service float plane to a very remote location. The rain came the next day and help end the fire season. We had prepared to canoe back to Ely, but we were picked up the day long light rain.

Our finances got to be difficult, summers often meant periods of homelessness. The way Kim and I dealt with the inability to maintain housing was either spending the summer camped out or to stay with a friend until we were able to let the fire money come in and balance out the books.

Working at public transit help stabilize our finances and I appreciate the company that I had worked for in giving me the chance to maintain a large piece of my personality, that part from high school which is always driven to serve as a fire fighter.

1996 was one of the hardest years for income. Everything was going well for the most part well. August I was sent by the DNR back to Grand Rapids to help lead another squad to in out of state fire. My crew would be sent to the Spring Fire in the Boulder Creek Wilderness Area 30 mile northwest of Crater Lake.

It was beautiful in the Oregon Mountains; I had been trying to set up a file with the county for my daughters so I could send letters and small gifts too. For the first eight years I had been denied every chance to set up this file that had been guaranteed by law. It still was about providing for the mother, not the fathers. **"Deadbeat dads were just to forget about their kids once they are gone."**

Up to the Oregon fire assignment I had been paying off my back child support. The county had billed me for all the back child support up to the end of 1995. Even though my rights were terminated I was originally billed in full for the whole time period to include seven years past the TPR (Termination of Parental Rights) order.

The county worker I spoke to once I was able to verify that my rights were terminated stated **"They will stop the payments only when the county was satisfied."** The county pulled nearly $4,000.00 beyond what was owed. I looked at the idea of returning to court for visitation rights when the county paid the excess back, the problem was even with the county misconduct no lawyer would **"Jeopardize their career for a deadbeat father."**

I would have rather continued to pay child support rather than to remain divided from my daughters.

Still while on the fire I wrote my letters to my daughters and mailed them to county social services uncertain what would happen next. We had other issues to worry about.

Once we arrived to our fire camp two hand crews were held from the fire line. Large clumps of ash were falling from the sky, still hot to the touch. The main smoke column was directly over our head. Command was preparing to move the camp; they just needed to figure out where would be the next safe place to camp a 6000 man fire camp.

By mid-afternoon they found a location, it was a forest service airstrip in the mountain. Word came to pack up the camp. We packed every vehicle that was there with supplies. Crew buses were loaded up with cases of MRE's (Meals Ready to Eat), hoses and hand tools. We packed everything except the cans of gas and the demolition cord.

Forest Service supply would come back to get it once the fire danger had pasted since the fire was too close to the road for safe transport.

We got into camp late and I was very tired, too tired to eat. It was a bad mistake not to eat supper. Morning came without a kitchen crew, no breakfast for the fire fighters until two hours later than expected. At the old camp we had a convict kitchen crew from Oregon department of Corrections, they didn't make the move with us to the new camp and the contract crew did not show up until late in the morning thinking their first serving was supper.

The next problem was environmentalist. To prevent logging in the wilderness area environmentalist had embedded railroad spikes into many of the trees in an effort to prevent logging of a wilderness area. However the spikes killed the trees with an overdose of iron and by the time of the fire the dead trees were hollow and fire would climb the inside and spread sparks beyond our reach and made the fire hard to control and even more dangerous.

The other problem was a picket line at an intersection near the fire camp. Forest fire fighting is more management of the fire rather than the complete suppression of the fire. Fire in the wilderness is actually a good thing when the weather conditions allow.

A century of over aggressive fire suppression plan has created a deadly over growth of
understory. Shrubs and fine grasses are the kindling that heats the large fuels and creates the movement of the fire. Add hot dry conditions and steep slopes and the fire becomes a living breathing hungry beast. Safety is paramount.

Our main objective was to protect infa-structure and property, secondary is allowing the fire to burn the wilderness properly and without a loss of life.

The problem comes with the need of using gas powered

pumps and saws to safely conduct our duties. The railroad spiked snags (dead standing trees) were a very big hazard on this fire. With a river on the southern edge we had a consistent water supply to aid with the fire fighting.

Basically command determines were they want the fire to be contained at and were to let it move to. As fire fighters we try to make the plan work. Without the power equipment the job would take longer and would become too dangerous. We made every attempt to preserve and protect the environment and in the case of this fire, 10,000 year old artifacts were to be protected as well.

All around the fire we would find stacks of rock, call prayer stacks. These prayer stacks were created by Native Americans in solace or as small groups in prayer sessions with the Great Spirit. Maybe to mourn the passing of a loved one, our for a good hunt or harvest either way we were told that this area that the fire was in had been used as a trading point for all the tribes in the pacific northwest to gather at.

Some of these prayer stacks were believed to be over 10,000 years old.

The terrain was very steep and our drop point was usually at 1 mile elevation and we would go between a half a mile below or even above that drop point elevation. We all got a work out and it lasted for three weeks.

Once home Kim and I moved to a small apartment. I gave some of our stuff animal collection to the fire department. Though I did try to join I was turned down.

On my return home I found my letters that I had sent to county social services for my daughters returned to me, but I was also given a case worker through a private adoption agency. Were things finally going to turn around? It was looking that way, but it wouldn't last.

Sunday night before Thanksgiving I woke to a very painful stomach. I tried a glass of milk, no good and I couldn't go to the bathroom. On physical exam I realize I had a serious problem, everything was looking at appendicitis. Kim has never been able to get a driver licenses due to her medical needs, I had learned from working rescue and ambulance, if you're the one who is sick do not be the one how is doing the driving. I called 9/11.

As an Emergency Medical Technician I felt the scene was stable enough, I have caught it early so no need for light and siren, no need for rescue I just need an ambulance to get to the hospital. So once the first police officer arrived to the apartment I requested that rescue be cancelled and the ambulance continued routine.

Once at the hospital the emergency room doctor tried everything to deny that I was having appendicitis. It was a fight and a half just to get the blood work done to verify the condition, or to even get my blood to drawn.

Once the white blood cell count came back I was on my way to surgery. I just would get there until 5 pm 17 hours after the start of the stomach pain, with no let up and now relief to the pain and discomfort. Part came from the fact I would not take the harsh pain killers, I wanted to be able to monitor the pain and didn't want to have to fight the additional side effects some medicines can cause.

Another concern that I had was in rehabilitation, knowing that the stomach can take more time for an individual over 30 to heal and I make a living by staying in great physical fitness. All I focused on was being ready for next year's fire season. Once out of surgery I was ready to get up and have a short walk, I was also very hungry.

Several of the nurses that were assigned to me that night were former nurses that I had worked with, it was great to see them and we caught up on our lives and were life has taken us.

Our family doctor came into visit as well. He wasn't happy that it took such an argument to get the ER doctor to do the proper blood work, and that the E.R. doctor didn't respect the fact that I was well trained in medical skills and would not had just shown up on a whim.

Craig's main concern, he knew my level of personal drive; and was afraid I would push too hard and create a greater injury while I was healing.

I was going to be off work for almost a month without any pay other than what Kim made as a bus aid, but her asthma was getting worst. I was sent home the night before Thanksgiving, I was already walking laps around the nursing station.

Once home I would spend the next two weeks taking daily walks in the community. We had gotten a cane for Kim since she always had a problem with falling, but she never used it. Now I needed it.

One day as I walk down the street the rescue squad passed by and I watched as the Lieutenant in the passenger seat pointed his finger and me and started laughing. To this day I do not know what that was about; we had many problems with him throughout the years to come. I had better things to focus on instead of what I had just witnessed, right at this moment it was to heal.

JANUARY 1997

The year opened up with a shock. I had several meeting with a worker at the private adoption agency regularly. My intent was to have a better relationship with social services so when my daughters came of age there would be an open path to allow for reunion and communications. What happened next was a cross from a prayer answered and the whole plan collapsing on its self.

I had been picking up a blind man in the Cretan Vandalia neighborhood of St. Paul. He had been staying in a house there as he took a jobs class for visual impaired to help him with the recent loss of his eye sight.

We had talked about life and family; I always talked about my daughters. I had this strong feeling whenever I picked him up that my daughters were nearby. He tried for nearly six months to accomplish this training he was taking in Minneapolis, but the transportation services unreliability and general human impatience took their toll on him and he moved back to Pine City.

Three weeks after he returned up north I had stopped at my bank in Inver Grove Heights and saw on the previous day's paper a picture of my daughters. Turned out their adopted mother had just graduated from the city of St. Paul's Police Academy. Their family was an expose' covered almost two whole pages. I had found my daughters. The date on the paper was January 7th

Over the previous Christmas Holiday my first wife had been calling my mothers telephone. With mom being out with family she was never home, but my first wife had left over 20 minutes of messages on the answering machine. She had spent the holidays in lockup and was soon going to a halfway house to rehabilitate. I had been able to find out where she was going to be at by calling the county services and explaining the problem. A meeting was set up.

Kim and Nick accompanied me to the meeting at the halfway house. We met in the basement which was set up as a recreation area. Her social worker was there as well and she came downstairs were an old fur coat. It was hard to believe that I was once married to her. We made our introductions, explained why we were there and played the tape from my mom's answering machine. I stopped it just seconds from before the point where she said her name in the tape. She was getting agitated and I wasn't there for a fight and was there to try to put a stop to a very big problem.

As we left, Nick told me that I did a really good job keeping my composure. Kim on the other hand said **"Now I remember when I first met you."** Nick and I both turned to her. **"I was walking into the shopping mall when this woman tried to attack me. I still remember the guy working so hard to keep us all apart and basically had to push her and the kids out the door."**

POST ADOPTION SERVICES REALLY
ISN'T THERE FOR FATHERS

At the adoption agency I was assigned a worker who claimed that she had a relationship with my daughters adopted family. It seemed like I had been developing a good idea to try to forge a positive relationship in hopes to encourage a healthy reunion once the girls reached age.

However when I found out where the girls live I contacted their agency and was referred to another social worker and this one had her own ideas.

We had an emergency meeting. It was one of the most hostile meetings I would ever have with a social worker. This new worker proclaimed that she; **"Was a product of a Wham, Bam, Thank You Ma-am and as far as she was concerned there are no such thing as a caring birth father just a bum and scum with a trick up his sleeve waiting for a chance to hurt or exploit his children. Besides what men only care about is sex anyways. What does a man really care about his children? You men are a problem and a burden and we would be better without you worthless men."**

Crushed doesn't even come close to how I felt when I left

that meeting, betrayed would be an understatement. The meeting ended with hostility from both sides, I could expect no more services from the adoption agency. Within two years they would send back all the gifts and letters I had filed there for my daughters through their services.

Spring came and I was ready for both the Army semiannual PT Test and the mile and half run I had to do for the DNR to stay on the call when needed roster. I missed out of pumps and chainsaw classes though, but was able to attend advance fire fighter training.

Kim would work with a social worker from another county, her son Jimmy had gotten into some trouble and some communication was allowed. There was a meeting and just a short period of communications, but what wasn't accomplished between my daughters and I was with Kim and her oldest boy Jimmy. We wouldn't enjoy the full fruit of this effort for a few more years to come, but the stage was set.

Back in the metro area we were having fires all over the place. The DNR opened a severity station at one of the county fire stations. I had been called in to help and had met one of the fire fighters at the station; he had been running the truck by himself and was pretty beat up for the day.

We went to fill the truck up with gas we noticed a plume of smoke rising from a housing development that was behind the gas station we went to investigate.

What we found was two 1 acre yards burnt black with active flames leaving the area and heading into an old landfill. The home owner was running around in bare feet trying to put the fire out with his garden hose. I had identified myself and that I was from the DNR and asked what had happened. He explained that they have a gopher problem and he had poured gasoline into the holes and lit a match. There was a burning ban in effect at the time.

I asked were the septic tanks for the two houses were so the trucks that would be coming in would damage them as we deal with the fire. He refused to let us enter his property the other fire fighter let him know if the fire enters the landfill he will have no choice.

So we watched as he put the complete fire out himself in his bare feet, we took his information and filled out the paperwork once back at the station.

Then there was massive flooding in the Red River Valley and the guard would eventually call for me to report to Camp Ripley. We then to convoy through Ada and finally to Hendrum, Minnesota were we stayed the night then sent home taking a convoy on no longer needed equipment with us.

I was prepared to stay three weeks instead I had only three days of state active duty. There I had caught up with some of my DNR friends who were functioning as incident managers.

During the summer we went to a fire north of Hoyt Lakes, Minnesota that bordered one of the iron mines. As we worked the fire as thunderstorms would build overhead. There were several mad scrambles to the vehicles as the lighting dropped from the sky around us. With the iron on the ground we found ourselves on a lightning rod.

For the most part we kept a large fire out of the news and the rest of the year was fairly uneventful. By fall I would return to college.

By spring of 1998 I would be part of a Heliattack Crew for the DNR and would start flying out of the Forest Lake Airport. Riding the helicopters provided one of the best experiences as a fire fighter. We could size up the fire before landing and we would be to so many more fires than I would ever be on with a truck. The program was growing and changing and I was a part of it.

I wouldn't make any of the out of state fires for 1998; just the same I had been to my share just with Heliattack and the engine alone. One weekend we had 24 solid hours of fire fighting running from one fire to the next.

We went from Forest Lake to Maple Grove with several fires in between. Our area lead fire fighter and I were in the lead truck and we found ourselves more than once trying to pinch down the head of a fire. When attacking a wildland fire the last place you want to be is working the fires head, it is unpredictable and dangerous even for experienced fire fighters and in the history of forest fires this is the place where many deaths have occurred. When I asked why we kept finding ourselves on the fire head he looked, winked and smiled, he felt safe with us working together.

Monday I was back at my regular job, but a big fire had broken out in Andover and the smoke could be seen from all over the metro area. Kim wouldn't let me report into the DNR office until I took her to the bank first, which was on the other side of the cities and through rush hour traffic as well. So I missed the fire, when we watched the news that night Kim stated she should had let me called the DNR first, the bank trip could had waited a day.

I had taken my cue from the social worker that worked with Kim, I wrote a letter to my daughter's adopted mother asking for a chance to stop somewhere and have a coffee together.

What I got next was a restraining order. The girl's family was told that I had been found guilty of abusing them and I also found out that the worker from the adoption agency had reported to them that I had made a threat of kidnapping in our heated meeting in January 1997.

Even though in that meeting when she had asked if I had indented any harm to my daughters, I had declined. Her word her title was all the evidence she needed as she made the false report.

I allegedly had a long police record of alcohol and domestic violence complaints and now my daughters where afraid for their lives of me. Funny thing was for the past year and a half whenever work took me near their home I would see them playing in the driveway.

Not once did I ever had approached them or found myself tailed or pulled over by a police officer. I simply wrote the letter with full of heartfelt honesty.

They also claimed to have a letter alleging that in 1992 I was having an affair with a teacher from a local school district and had used her to attempt to contact the girls through their oldest son. No letter has presented, they stated they could bring it if asked.

I attempted to present my actual police record and the judged refused it saying "**I don't need that.**" I would be simply pushed out of the courtroom with no value in anything I tried to say or present the courts mind had already been made before the trial even begun.

I had filed complaints against both social workers through the Board of Social Workers. The Board finally had the authority to review complaints against county works simply for the main reason he now had a licenses. However any facts that the complaint was based on was viewed of as a lack of objectivity and what laws were broken by either social workers where outside of the scope of the Minnesota Board of Social Workers enforcement. Nothing more would be done by the state, otherwise there was no real standard of care for social workers in Minnesota.

In other words the board is there to prevent sexual abuse between clients and the workers and nothing else.

The only good that came from it was that the one social worker was forced to take an early retirement from private adoption agency for her miss handling of my case, but I was still not allowed any means to develop a positive connection with my daughters and no other worker stepped forward to help assist with the manners of this situation. The silent divide continued. Even the original worker refused anymore meetings with me.

In the news residential yards are being dug up on the belief that a child remain would be found there. Repressed Memory Syndrome what the big word for the day and a mental health profession had convinced the county to arrest the father and dig up the yard for the alleged remains.

It turned out to be an act of fraud by a leading County Child Protection contract mental health agency worker. The psychiatrist would be found guilty for the crime license revoked and sent to prison. I worried if the she had been the one that my daughters may have used.

Another issue came in the form as an open letter to the people by the famous child development expert apologizing for he had finally married a lady half his age and with a teenage daughter who proceed to prove his theories wrong. He was fully aware with the number of family dismantle with county agencies quoting his theories in tow. He did more harm than good and by the year's end he would pass from this earth.

Also in the news was the news released from the very county that took my parental rights away of a 30 years parental study that showed single fathers had nearly as good of an effort in raising healthy and well developed kids as dual parent families. Single mothers had a dismal showing even though the belief remained that the kids needed to stay with their mothers.

Another issue came when a mother killed her six kids by drugging them and drowning each of them one at a time in a bath tub. The media stated the same old claim of the worthlessness of the fathers. They married in a refugee camp under the cultural traditions.

By the time her family made to United States with tribe was broken apart and the mother had fallen apart from not only her family, the tribe and county social services as well. The county had isolated the family and even though the dad repeated pressed concerns for the children's safety. County social services still doesn't listen to fathers specially those who relocated with traditions social services doesn't support.

We heard it in the news and I heard it the next day when I was transporting a county foster grandparent who blast us damn fathers. **"The world was going to be better without those deadbeats in the families."** I told her my story and she went silent as I dropped her off she told me she would pray for my family.

The following months would bring the whole failure to light. Regardless how old the tradition was the behavior of county social services is what killed those kids. They refused to investigate simply by a false ideology that failure to investigate and taken the seriousness of the needs that mother had. The idea that women could never commit any violent crime, violent crime was only a man thing was undeniably proven false.

She stood less than 5 feet and under 100 pounds. She had found the way to free her from her children. It brought back memories. The feeling of the abandonment when county social services made me walk the walls with no one not even the county board would offer an ear or a concern. I felt the painful pit in my stomach 10 years after I walked the county halls another father made the same walk to the same apathetic ideas that claimed both of us as a flaw to society.

PARTY LIKE ITS 1999

For the summer of 1999 Kim and I took Kay's son Josh for the summer. He had just turned 14 and the kid's behavior had caused them to be evicted from their apartment. Jenna was in foster care and since Kay didn't have a car Kim and I would pick up Jenna from the foster home and return her each weekend.

When Kay and the kids got evicted she sent all the kids but Larissa to anyone that could take them for the summer as she found a new place and got settled in.

Josh began showing some alarming difficulties. He had failed school and needed to take summer classes but he was having outbursts of violence and has threatening other kids and creating property damage. We had on several occasions found the need to make a police report.

Then in July I received a phone call from the DNR, they needed help looking for the remains of Katie Poirer. I prepared for the grim task of the next day, and then the telephone rang again, **"Standby, you may be going to the Boundary Waters Canoe Area instead."** A storm had passed through the BWCA falling over 100,000 acres of trees and stranding and trapping campers. If they couldn't get everyone accounted for over night then was in the BWCA we were to join the search otherwise it would be to Moose Lake, Minnesota to look for Katie.

Josh had caused Kim a load of troubles at home; I had transferred to a local office of the bus company that I was working for. He was to call in each day for his ride to school and this day he refused to make the call. Kim and our neighbor Jen went to Bingo to give Kim a needed break from Josh's actions. I arrange Josh's bus for the next morning then Josh tried to turn against me.

I simply ordered him into the push-up position in a Drill Sergeant fashion. I was encouraging him to do push-ups rather than to get into a heated argument with him. This list of things he did in the neighborhood that day would have locked him away for the rest of his childhood.

I had also opened my front door so that if anyone called the police they could simply step inside. Our cat Mischief, must have figured out that this was going to get ugly, he scampered to the back bedroom and jumped up on the bed.

Within minutes an out of breath police officer would appear at the door. I looked at him and said, **"Your, turn."** And went outside and waited for the squad to show up. When the squad arrived the police officer had me stand facing the squad car, waiting for the word to put hand cuffs on me. He would not take any statements from me at all I had to be the guilty party.

The police officer came out of our house and to his partner simply said **"Your, turn. I need to talk to this one."** He had me turn around and asked if I knew how loud my voice really was. He had ran a distance of greater than four blocks thinking someone was getting killed.

What that first police officer found at the door an adult male standing over a 14 year old boy in the push-up position, and trying to convince him to take better responsibility for himself. He said at no time did the volume of my voice changed. The volume stayed at the same volume as he first heard through his whole run.

The police reaffirmed the risk Kim and I had taken for Josh

and that he really needed to try better for himself. That if he continued on his current path the facility in Lino Lakes wasn't too far from a possibility.

We started talking about everything that was going on, I let him know I am also feeling some stress for what I may have to do the following day. Both stories were well known in the news and neither of them I was looking completely forward to, but I would do what was asked of me to do. Meanwhile for Josh we were trying to find some way to turn a boy around before it was too late.

Part of the problem was we were in contact with Kay's social worker; she made it very difficult to report any of the problems we were seeing, just ridicule us for taking the boy since we couldn't handle him. That was why we ended up making police reports instead, it was the only means and after this evenings event the police were in line to help us with the task because they too were receiving complaints of Josh's behavior and were also struggling with what to do.

The next morning I reported in to the DNR and the crew went to Moose Lake to join the search for Katie. The suspect was already in jail and confessed to her kidnapping, rape, and murder. We were trying to find anything left from her cremated remains. I was sickened to the idea that the suspect had been returned to his family over eight times after pleading guilty to all sorts of abuse to the young girls of his family and their friends.

Now we walk in a line often through brush so thick we could only move touch shoulder to shoulder. My voice was gone from the previous nights affairs so to either side of me were fire fighters that had also serviced in the military and all we needed to do was hand signals until my voice got better.

Of all the fire fighters there I wore a red baseball cap that I got from my guard unit for helping with the Expert Field Medical Badge Testing during annual training.

I had earned the badge back in 1983 when I was in Germany I was part of the cadre. Everyone else hats were blue, saw each night my hat would be seen going into the woods on the local news.

We found bags of torn clothes and pile of bones all over the place. The bones were of deer most likely hunted by wolves, but some could have been hunter waste piles, left to decay or be consumed by the wildlife. It was a long week of early morning briefings, TV news crews, and shoulder to shoulder walking.

Much of the land in this part of Minnesota is a combination of sandy out cropping of trees and brush with swampy areas in between with soft ground opening of areas of water. One step could be on solid ground the next step would be waist deep in water.

The one nice thing of this search was the fact many changes had occurred in dealing with Post Traumatic Stress and the development of the Critical Incident Stress Debriefing.

Gone were the days of simply sucking it up, drink it out of you, or stuff the feelings in so deep till you break. On the last day we would spend over an hour looking at what we had just experienced and how theses traumatic incidents can shape us.

Still that one hour for me wasn't enough.

It was blessed to be in a National Guard medical unit that had a behavioral science section. The next morning from the search I had let my platoon sergeant know that I was going to need sometime. However what was I thought going to be a 15 minute ordeal took most of the morning and didn't clear out until lunch time.

I was hurting to the fact of everything I was being put through with my daughters and here the guy who committed this heinous crime was given so many chances to have his family always near him and even with the current events he was not going to lose his parental rights. Compounding the problem, he had a niece serving in my national guard medical company. So I had the chance to verify some of the information we were told.

The process of the Katie Poirier Search only made my quest for my daughters even more driven.

August the DNR would send us to the BWCA to assist with recovery efforts in the Blow Down Event. It was amazing to see piles of trees, still with leave fluttering in the wind, piled on top of each other. Some piles were over 40 feet high. Our primary task was to open the Banadan Cross Country Ski Trail.

We spent the week living at the End of the Trail Resort at the very end of the Gunflint Trail. Dropping off at a drop point we would hike into the storm damage. For the most part we would have sections of trail unaffected by the storm damage only to go over a hill or around a turn and face a wall of debris. Chain saw operators would first release the stump ball from the trees to release the weight of the soil on the rest of the fallen trees.

The BWCA is an area of shallow soil some areas were the trees were knocked over it was the tress root system that created the ground cover, lichen grew across the roots and grass grew from the lichen. The dead grass and moss would produce the soil for more plants to grow in. In a nut shell most of the area had less than a ½" of actual soil the rest were the tree roots and plant life.

If the trees were to be cut without removing the root ball first the part of the trees not yet cut what becomes a catapult and anyone on it would be thrown through the air. So the job started with spotting the sawyer and make sure he could safely remove the weight of the root system first before removing the rest of the tree from the trail.

Against the wishes of the environmentalist we were using chain saws since that really was the only safe way to accomplish the task. Our job was to return the public access to the BWCA, not to harvest any of the trees felled by the storm.

Once the summer was done I was back to college.

I had for the second time tried to join the local volunteer fire department, only to be turned away. They wanted to honor my old fire chiefs' actions in forcing me off the fire department. The old fire department turned me down as well, even though I lived less than four minutes from one of their other stations.

One fall day I was coming home from school I could see a

thick column of smoke in the distance. As I got closer to home I realized that it was very close to work. We had a boy over trying to get my computer to work right. I had to get him home before I got to work. The fire turned out to be almost next door to my office was, I picked up my bus and went out on my route. I had a three day weekend coming up so I called the DNR dispatch and the next day reported into the fire office to assist with the fire.

There were four fires that made up the incident. The two biggest fires were located on the north and south ends of the fire area, with the largest being next to the bus company office I was working for. One of the smallest fires was located near the fire chief's house. These fires all started very close together and everyone expressed a concern that these fires had to have been started by a fire fighter.

Saturday the two large fires were still actively burning. I set up a watering point on Main Street for the trucks that were working the fire and delivered the equipment needed for an Anoka County Sentence to Serve Crew to lay out a hose line from a pond to help keep the fire away from some houses. Many of my former fire fighters were happy to see that I too was still fighting fires, some were not happy at all. Still we worked the fire for the weekend and the fire was out in time to go back to school.

I was plugging along with school and work when our bathroom floor gave way one day under Kim. My attention was now returned to our immediate needs and the fact we were only a pay check away from homelessness. School would again have to wait and I would become delayed in going back to school.

In the family law legislation Minnesota would pass a bill into law that would require new father's to claim their parental rights over their child within 30 days of the child's birth. New fathers at the guard unit were stating how they were actually being trick to sign the rights away to the mother as they were required to sign the paperwork.

Josh on the other hand when he moved back in with his mother had gotten mad at her and dislocated her shoulder. He would spend the rest of his childhood in the very system I was trying to redirect him from.

Fire season for the spring of 2000 would start early. I was getting ready for another three day weekend when again at work I witnessed a huge plume of smoke develop

As fire trucks from 5 different fire departments and the DNR would respond, March came in with the dragon. A high school student who slipped out to have a quick cigarette set the swamp behind the high school. The next day I would be on the DNR engine and help mop the fire up.

There was still ice embedded in the moss of the bog. It just wasn't enough ice and the exposed upper layer had thawed and dried out in the weeks of sunshine prior to the fire. Signs around us indicated that this fire burned very hot and we were lucky that is didn't involve any of the houses that surrounded this swampy area. The weekend was spent mopping up hot spots.

A contractor arrived with some heavy equipment to help dig out the deep hot spots that the smoldering moss created. By June I would be hired by this contractor who responded to all sorts of disasters and cleaned parking lots and did landscaping in between. I was actually pressured by the manager to quit my job with the bus company and I put in a resignation without a two week notice.

I was hoping to arrange it in a way that if I needed the bus job again I would have it, but the manager really didn't give me much choice. I was getting paid more and doing the work that I identify myself with.

First job was to go to northern Wisconsin on a severity assignment. The fire risk was high so extra engines and aircraft were staged in case a wildfire broke out. This help the contractor set up the federal fire contract and we had a good time in Wisconsin touring the Nicolette National Forest until the spring rains finally came. I have often quoted I should be hired a rain maker since every time I get on a severity assignment it usually rains within a week.

Once back to Minnesota I am set up for parking lot sweeping. Before that job took off I was called in early to go water lawns and be part of a roll off tanker and track vehicle that was set up as well for fire response. Then we were sent to a fire assist call instead.

The fire is located in a swamp that has housing area to the west and open grassland, swamp and trees within. The land was part of an old sod farm and we work the fire late into the night. Salvation Army provided hot dogs for supper and again I find myself working with the fire fighters I had once worked with, a lifetime ago. During the fire I would lose a Gerber folding knife in the fire and would never find it.

The next day I was sweeping parking lots in a small vacuum sweeper truck that was painted purple. The short nose trucks had a great turning radius and were fun to drive. I could dance the truck to the music on the radio. However within three weeks the next disaster job would wind up. Eagan was hit with a very powerful storm and we were sent to help mitigate the damage.

We pulled into the housing project area to find most of the new homes in this construction projects flooded out. One house the foundation gave way and the concrete was nearly pushed against the basement ceiling, a fine mud covered everything. We went into one house and pulled out a water logged sofa.

Four of us carried it up a hill and to the street as the Channel 5 News helicopter circled above us. For the rest of the year we were part of the station's news commercial. For the rest of the month of June we worked the project, not worrying about what happening in the politics of the job just doing the best job we could do. for the city of Eagan and its residents.

One part of the job was to place a soil stabilization pad on a part of one road that had weakened for all the water. We made the pads ourselves and delivered them to the site, anchoring to the ground. In the process the crane operator struck a gas line that was not marked properly. We abandoned the site and secured off the road to keep people out of harm's way and called 911. Police and fire were glad to see that the scene was properly secured and waited with us for the gas company to arrive. This line we struck was a main service main 12" in diameter. Our quick actions prevented a calamity; too bad some of the neighbors didn't like the interruption of their life. One gentleman demanded that we reopen the street and wanted to argue, we referred him to the police car that had parked at the intersection keeping cars from going down the street. We never heard from him again.

Before this job was completed the company was part of a resource order to eastern Idaho for fire severity. In the Idaho High Desert the fire danger reached the extreme level larger fires were already burning in the Salmon Challis National Forest. Three small trucks were en route to Idaho Falls with the support of a Minnesota DNR heavy engine.

After check in we were sent to the hotel and the next morning we staged in a park in downtown Idaho Falls. The first fire we were sent to was at the USDA Sheep Research Station in Dubois, Idaho. It was the second day of the fire and everything was in mop up.

Still as we pulled up we were brief that this was a lighting strike fire that had destroyed a research project. The researcher from the University of Oregon was studying the **"Sexual motivations of homosexual rams."** Yes, that is how it was described.

The researcher claimed he had been given a 1.5 million dollar federal research grant for this project. I wouldn't have the full story behind his study until years later. At the time we took the fire as an act of God, an expression of a higher beings opinion of the study.

Still we were on the fire and we split up into two teams, the two trucks I was with did a slow sweep of the western part of the fire line and put out hot spots we found along the way.

The other trucks went to the northern parts and worked their way along the eastern part of the line. They got to see all the sheep that were killed by the fire, on my side of the line we didn't have to have that view.

By late afternoon a cold front developed and thunderheads formed very quickly. I told my driver let's get to the road and we parked behind a bulldozer. The rest of the crews were still working their way out of the fire when the sky erupted in lighting.

The virga curtain was high in the sky, no rain would ever hit the ground not matter how heavy it was raining in the upper atmosphere, and it crossed over us with only a coating mist of rain on the trucks.

On the valley below we could see numerous smoke columns develop were we witness lightning strikes on the ground. The valley below was quickly filling with smoke. The bull dozer driver was talking to dispatch as crews were scrambling to get to the fires were. He called us to follow him and off we went.

First we started to head to one fire and was told to instead turn around and got to another. The fire we went to was the smaller of the big one developing to the south, with luck our fire would be out in the evening and we would join the crews working the larger fire. The bigger fire was caused by several lighting starts burning together into one large fire.

That night we camped in Dubious.

"DO YOU REMEMBER THE MOVIE CHINA SYNDROME?"

We spent the first week working in and out of Idaho Falls. By the second week a fire camp had been established at the Pocatello, Idaho High School. For the next three week we camped there, before moving to the fairgrounds.

Before being assigned to Fort Hall we were dispatched to the Hawkins Reservoir Fire. This fire was an arson fire that moved quickly through both a steep topographic forest land and harvested wheat field fields. The ranchers drove their large tractors hard creating a wide path of over turned soil so that the fire would come across the fields and threaten the town of Downey. We arrived just hours before sunset and took our position on the tail of the fire. First job was to make the brunt area meet the fire line, any pocket of grass and woody plants would be burnt.

Jason my driver nearly stepped on a rattle snake that is now attached to his boot, unable to release its' fangs from the thick heal of the logging boots. There are holes all over the ground making walking difficult. One of our trucks wasn't refueled in the morning like it was to. The driver didn't take the time to prep the truck and was reckless in his handling of the vehicle. We needed to get the trucks off the line and fueled before continuing, since only one person controlled the credit card we all had to go together.

At the convenience store of our fire fighters asked the locals about the holes, in a heavy drawl the reply was **"Them, there are badger holes. They'll tear you up."** We all about fell over in laughter. The locals noticed that we were from Minnesota and all the sudden we were surround with Minnesota Viking fans.

We would work the fire for five days one of the biggest memories of this fire was the dust devils of pure soot that would hang in the center of fire all day. It would start about 10 am and stay there until just before sunset. Never moving from the spot, just rotating in place, it was huge and went into nothing but clear sky. A local newspaper posted a picture of it in a local paper.

We could had walked up and touched it if we weren't so busy trying to get the fire out.

Over a month we would be staged at Fort Hall Indian Reservation and be sent to the fires from there. One fire was to the located in a place called the Idaho National Engineering and Environmental Laboratory. The fire there would have an exclusion zone that we could not enter, not even to chase the fire. We had a line in the sage brush that we couldn't cross.

We were briefed in what the INEEL does for the Department of Energy and were met with a statement that the movie **"China Syndrome"** was loosely based on an accident that had happened there. The INEEL develops the safety procedures for all the nuclear reactors in the United States, including the Nautilus Submarines. We were screened given radiological safety badges and escorted onto the property.

After the fire was put out we washed the trucks, cleaned out the air filters and were screened for radiation before they took us to their dining facility for supper. We returned to our main fire camp late into the night for bed.

We were in Idaho for over 65 days, I had a guard uniform sent and I did a weekend drill with the Idaho National Guard in Pocatello. I was also approached by one of our fire fighters while we spent time in Montpelier, Idaho pulled me aside.

Larry stated that he had been involved as part of a police reserve program for Columbia Heights and that during the past year they were called into Fridley to assist with the arrest of a Social Worker who had been discovered falsify and destroying case documents.

He knew a lot about me, more than what most people knew. He knew about the day of the plane crash when I had the chance I went to the scene briefly and had gotten in trouble for that. Keeping the siren going was not even a consideration, but to leave my post even if properly relieved did not give me a reason to check the scene out. I had learned about self discipline on the fire department.

He knew many things about the case, being escorted out of the state capital when the attorney general's office blew me off. Of all the years of lobbying for father rights and always searching for the chance to right a serious wrong and be reunited with my daughters.

He even asked what I was doing in the day I stood watch over a professional wrestling match and what was I thinking getting involved with Karen and her boys. He said you have guts and we are glad for what you have done and we prayed that my daughters would turn around and give me a chance.

In all we went to over 12 fires in eastern Idaho and time came for the drive home. By now the company had accumulated 9 pick truck size brush engines, 4 heavy trucks and trailers, all terrain vehicles and even bought a few broken down trucks there it was time to bring it all home.

What a convoy that was and it took two days to get home with a night in Butte, Montana and Bismarck, North Dakota. All these white fire trucks in a line heading back to Minnesota.

Once home it was back to sweeping parking lots and weekend Heliattack for the DNR. The parking lot work was four day on and four days off so I had plenty of time to help during the hot dry fall to ride the helicopter. Mid-October we would face our biggest metro area fire yet.

The weather forecast called for a dramatic change in the winds by mid afternoon. The winds came early. The first call came in around 10 am for a fire in the Staples area. It was a small fire started by an arsonist. We flew in and put it out.

As the refueler for the helicopter did his job we had the bird ready for the fire we could already hear dispatches for additional fires that were spring up all over the northern metro area. Then the radio asked for our status, we had another fire to report to.

The second fire was in East Bethel, a careless cigarette thrown into a harvested corn field setting it on fire and the winds were picking up. As we lifted from the scene of the first fire, reports of a third fire was coming in.

The Carlos Edge Fire sprang to life. We flew hard across two counties to get to our assigned fire. We could see both smoke plumes, and the wind was picking up to over 20 mph.

As we touched down on our assigned fire we knew that the third fire was still small yet building rapidly. Carlos Edge Fire was caused when a legal burn rekindled in the wind and the fire left the private property that the burn was done and quickly spread into the Carlos Avery Wildlife Refuge. First we had to get our fire our so we could join the fight.

Fire equipment throughout the northern suburbs and DNR offices were being dispatch Carlos Edge was growing larger at an alarming rate. What resources that were on the scene the fire had already been passed by the fire without any affect of the fire fighters actions.

Back at our fire we worked at a break neck pace to put it out and get to the bigger fire. Our fire was small and contained we needed to make sure it didn't rekindle or become large enough to join the larger fire. We knocked out fire out of a pine wind break and once the active flames were out the engine relieved us to go to the bigger fire. They would follow once this fire was completely out. The helicopter was needed Carlos Avery. The pilot waved off the refueler, he would meet him at the larger fire we packed the Bambi Bucket climb on board and lift off. The helicopter blades never stopped spinning.

As we lifted over the tree line a soft profanity was heard in the headset, as the helicopter turned to the Carlos Edge Fire a large column of smoke filled the windshield. The beast was alive and the fire had all the momentum. We did our required lap around the fire as our heliattack manager made his report to the Incident Commander

Our radios came alive with the sounds of fire department pager tones, by now every Anoka and Chicago County fire departments were en route heading to this one fire.

We touched down on a flat piece of land that was just shy of the fire's point origin. As our helicopter took off to start the bucket drops the Princeton, Minnesota landed behind him.

The two crews became one team, the heliattack managers hop scotch each helicopter to one hot spot to the next. Our little squad walked the same section of line to make sure the fire stayed out. It would take several trips. One of the DNR engines was stuck in the peat moss and would not move.

We grabbed any additional tools and bottles of water from the truck. The trucks crew was doing the same thing as we were on the southern part of the line.

The peat bog had been exposed when the water level dropped to more than over 6 feet below the normal water line for this area. At one point I fired up the pump on the truck because the peak was burning underneath it and threatening to damage the struck rig before it could get pulled out.

Shortly before sunset a small bulldozer appeared we pulled the truck out and the crew was relieved to see that they didn't have to wait for the tow. Aircrews for forest fire fighting rarely stay out over sunset. After all the planes and helicopters left for the night my helicopter had to make one final lap for the Incident Commander, our hearts sunk when following the fires edge we witness a house explode into flames as the fire consumed it.

Luckily no one was killed in this fire, but on the fires first day there were injuries and three houses were lost to the fire. From my house you could see the glow from the fire, over 20 miles away. I was too pumped from the day to go to sleep, Penny and Sammy were spending the night and I loaded them up in the Ford ranger I got on Memorial Day and gave everyone a quick look at the fire from a safe distance.

Fire trucks were still heading up Interstate 35 to reach the staging on Viking Drive and receive their assignments. I have never heard so many sirens in my life and they continued through the night and into the next day.

The following morning I reported to the Forest Lake Airport were the DNR had set up has our helibase. Our first assignment of the day was to prepare for three National Guard Helicopters that would operated from this little airport with a grass runway.

Once we marshaled the helicopters in we had a full helibase operations set up. Our first priority was to be available for any additional fires in the area. Second was to support the needs of the Carlos Edge Fire.

Once the National Guard was off with their assignments we ran up to the Community Center to set up a helispot for the Incident Commander. He was already using our helicopter to tour the fire and make the plan for the day. Most of the DNR engine crews had worked the fire over night without any sleep and now were in their second day.

The fire was pushing hard to the northeast, Interstate 35 was closed due to heavy smoke and the fears that the fire would jump the freeway and into the eastern unit of the refuge that is all peat bog and poor road access, the attempt was to hold the line. A large trailer park sat in the fires path.

We did get a dispatch for a fire that was started when an all terrain vehicle back fired. The field we landed on was met with some protest of the property owner. He didn't want us landing there. But it was the only spot close to the fire. He was directed to call the DNR. The fire was put out and we went back to the airfield.

At the day's end I for some reason could not remember where I had placed my car keys; the other fire fighter of our crew gave me a ride home. At arriving at the address we found a squad car rescue and an ambulance at my house. Kim had fallen through a floor vent while holding a little child. The child was unhurt but Kim could not move her knee.

I had the ambulance take her to the hospital as I grabbed the spare keys for the truck. As I was leaving a fire fighter was heard **"No wonder it take so many people to lift such a fat ###%%%."** I had to meet Kim at the hospital and the fire to our north was still burning without let up our control efforts were failing, I had too much to worry about some childish remarks of someone who just as big as my wife.

Three days later I was on the contract fire fighters engine, working the same fire. Over the weekend frost had set in and slowed the fires momentum enough to give fire fighters a chance to secure the line, the trailer park was saved. Now it was time to mopped it up and pick up the pieces.

The fire just missed the DNR fire base, yet nearly the entire west unit of Carlos Avery had been burnt and now the peat bog was all that was left to smolder. With populated areas all around the refuge it would be not be safe to keep the refuge smoldering and pray for enough snow for winter to finish the job. Flooding the swamp became the next task.

The engine I was on was supporting a North Carolina Hand Crew that was mopping up hot spots that surrounded the lower swampy areas. We had just moved nearly 1200 gallons of water through the pump when one of the fire fighters in the hand crew dropped his axe picking up tree debris and chopped into his boot. The cut to the foot was going to need stitches everyone on the line knew I was o medic and I did have enough supplies to treat the injury.

After treating the worker I returned to the truck to find the pump had ran out of gas and needed to be refueled. The gas can was stored behind the pump and was being difficult to recover. The truck also had a rounded rear bumper that added in the cause of me losing my footing and falling with my ungloved hand onto an unguarded muffler.

I immediately put my hand into the drop tank that the truck was parked against. My hand stung from the burn and I wanted to cool it before looking at it. I directed one of the other fire fighters to help refuel the pump and start it up. I reported my injury up the chain and the company manager brought a relief for me as he took me to the hospital.

I was mad, and livid. 25 years I have been in and around fire, never getting anything but minor injuries and even then that was far and few. Now I have I massive 2nd degree burn to my right hand and en route to the emergency room. I had also found out the unguarded muffler on the pump had burned six others and had never had a shield installed. All the burns were for the same reason losing footing trying to recover the gas can for the pump.

My next cycle for heilattack was coming up and my injury would keep me off the helicopter.

I would spend the rest of the time on the fire driving the hand crew on the short bus. The last day there I would assist the bulldozer on the fire. By the end of the day I would find out that the manager was putting equipment on the fire without the resource request from the DNR.

He had us do a bunch of work that the company would not get paid for.

Back at home I was poking around on our computer and found my oldest daughters' e-mail for the University of Minnesota. I sent her an e-mail. She responded with a restraining order. I was someone she never, ever wanted in her life. I no longer existed in her heart.

My daughter's adopted mother would e-mail me claiming that **"Since (her) father abandoned her at birth never to expect her to advocate the reunion of my daughters and me. In her** eyes I am no different than he was and should simply forget that they were ever mine. (I) was simply a waste of time"

The hearing in Duluth was different than what was going on back in the cities. Even though I brought the court records that I had copies of with all I got from the judge was **"Good luck"**, but still no effort to look at what was really going on nor any attempt to resolve this issue in manner that doesn't leave someone hurting.

I was losing options and as I left I heard her adopted brother state **"Do you think the idiot has finally learned his lesson."** My daughters were adopted into vanity, I was demoralized. All I wanted was to have the two most precious people in my life active in our relationship together not separated because someone found power by denying it.

As Kim and I returned to the cities the things I thought about was how much my daughter now looks and sounds like her mother. Kim was hurt over the remarks of the eldest son. I went and talked to several representatives and senators at the state capital.

At the state capital our elected representative was a joke. He wasn't going to put himself between the fathers and the mothers as far as he was concerned **"You fathers just need to give up when the mothers tell you to quit. And don't expect any support for fathers from me anyways you no longer needed in the family so get over it."**

At least my state senator would take the information and look at it with a more open set of eyes.

Back home and back to work. Winter came with vengeance and soon heavy snow fall was followed with record cold. I went from sweeping parking lots to shoveling sidewalks.

Right before I changed jobs from the bus company to the disaster mitigation company Kim's son Jimmy met back up with us and now he was living in Sauk County Wisconsin. My first question was who was he dating? He didn't have to try that hard to get into the family, but now he was in the seat of the family and in the Baraboo Trailer part that his girl friend and he shared my cousin was a maintenance man there.

We had a reason to make frequent trips to Wisconsin now and we would stop by with Jimmy and the relatives. We would also stop at my dads' grave. They were expecting a child and we all happily waited for Dayton's birth and spoiled him once he arrived. Jimmy's adopt parents got jealous.

One day Jimmy accidentally dropped Dada causing a bruise. No matter what he pleaded with his adopted parents we would never be allowed to see our grandchild while they are alive.

In their eyes regardless we were never fit to be a parent and even when we were showing that we were better people they look for reasons to control the situation. They just used the lost of our parental rights from the previous relationships as the only proof they needed to declare us as poorly as they did.

Actually we got along better with the mother, but the father was stubborn to his ideas and since they were retired psychologists they had the right to judge us as they saw fit. Once Kasota was born they moved Jimmy's trailer to Mankato and Jimmy and Jesse fell apart. Now the grandkids are brought to us in secret.

Kim and I have to again wait for the day that the kids decide what they want as the adopted grandparents used money and power to control the situation.

For a while Jimmy and I work together at the disaster company, it was for a period during an ice storm that plugged up the Northfield Target. Jimmy and Jessie lived nearby and we took shelter at their apartment to warm up. We never could keep up the ice until the storm past until morning and the road conditions became too dangerous to drive on so we spent the night between Northfield and their apartment in Faribault.

One heavy storm I had just got home from shoveling sidewalk and got called to bring the pumper to the scene of a serious train derailment. When I got to the office the truck was frozen. The hose in the bed was useless so I dumped it and got fresh hose. I checked the truck and put whatever equipment I could find.

Once on the scene I attempted to thaw out the plumping system. The last person who used the truck didn't drain the pump and the ice could have damaged the pump if the train derailment happened much later in the winter.

Instead I was sent to one of the nearby fire stations to clear the pump of ice and function test to make sure it would still work. What I didn't know was it was Pat's plan to send all the trucks to staging in hopes to bill for equipment sent but never used. He wasn't planning on the truck to be pressed into service.

The cold weather was taking the communities fire department equipment out faster than they could replace it. Trucks needed to be repair and brought back into the availability of the community.

Our truck fit the needs the railroad had control of the incident he sent a fire department representative and if our truck could work he could get his fire department back to protecting the community. It took three hours but after using up all the hot water in the station water flowed through the pipes of the old pumper and I was preparing it for a pump test.

A soon as it passed the test we brought back to the scene and switched the last city truck off the hydrant and I hook the company truck to the lines. Within minutes I started the longest watch of my life and by the time I was relieved I had spent over 40 hours on shift and had over 100 hours for the week.

The next time I would deal with the train derailment was while we were contracted to provide security over the wreckage since everything was now a solid block of ice. It would be until late march before the wreckage could be collected and the cars of what was once molten sulfur prepared for hazmat disposal.

The recovery process was to temporarily secure the wreckage to old flat bed cars that the railroad will throw away with the wreckage. However the debris had to be secured to the cars and the plan was to weld them permanently to the flatbeds and transport it all to the landfill and throw everything away. However welding creates heat and heat got the sulfur to start burning again. I was sent with another worker to keep the prep site fire safe.

It took almost two weeks to recover all 29 cars and prepare them for disposal. Shortly afterwards the company would send a large group of us to Crew Boss and Engine Boss Class and HAZWOPER and HAZMAT Technician class

By now spring fire season arrived and it lasted only one weekend was I spent on the helicopter again. This time we were based in Carlos Avery directly. As I left the helibase for the last time a funnel cloud was called out by a Skywarn watcher who was to my east. I confirmed the sighting by looking up and seeing the funnel right over my head. I called the funnel report over the Skywarn net and beat feet out of there. Seeking cover under a tree as it started to hail heavily and waited for the storm to pass.

I was set up for three annual trainings units were short medical staff as well as an Expert Field Medical Badge test was being conducted with our Iowa counterparts. Right before I was to report to the first annual training period the company manager would gamble and sent me as part of a three truck engine convoy to Florida in hopes that we could get a jump on the fires. We never had a Resource Order.

I split trained that months drill with the Florida National Guard and then was home at the end of the week.

The company got fined for interfering with my annual training. I reported to Camp Dodge, Iowa for the next round. While there two things would come to light. One was a story of an Iowa father suing Children's Home Society and the State of Minnesota for kidnapping.

It was filed as a class action suit however once checking with the district court in Minneapolis under the case number the page was missing and the court clerk would not provide any information, just two chad's of paper remained of the paperwork that was missing from the court docket folder. The clerks offered no advice.

The story as report from the Iowa newspaper was that the guys wife took off to Minnesota to have the child hidden from him until the required time period had passed for the child to be given up for adoption without any consent from the father.

32 days after the birth of his son mom called dad to gloat at what see had done. Some lawyers in Minnesota where stating **"That if he wanted his rights so badly he needed to actively search for her, if he couldn't find her maybe he wasn't looking hard enough."** Only one lawyer stood up and any chance for others that faced the same wickedness that the one sided policy had developed and the problems it was causing.

I would hear much later that the outcome of the trial was that the state supreme court ruled that fathers do not have protected rights within the state laws. Yet from what I saw sweeping changes where occurring, but they would be slow and other battles would be fought. Always showing we humans are short on memory long on blame.

SIREN TORNADO

A s the end of the Iowa annual training period a tornado struck a 41 mile path from the east end of Grantsburg to just south of Spooner, Wisconsin. Siren, Wisconsin was in the middle of its path. I barely got home when the manager was on the phone calling me to report to the scene. I had him wait until I was done completely with annual training before reporting into the Hugo office. I needed time to refit the bags and have some time with my wife.

I would bring a truck to the work site and take over a hook truck for the day picking 20 yard dumpster that were filled with debris. The next day I would be working as the company representative and liaison with the numerous volunteers that came to help.

The over the weekend a volunteer had collapsed from heat injury, now my job was to keep from happening again. The jobsite was massive I had driven from one side of the tornado zone to the other twice a day for nearly the next two months. The only break came for the Sunday afternoons and the short week spent in Albert Lea when the Farmland Pork Processing Plant caught fire, but more on that one later.

Working between the Burnett County Emergency Management

Team and the volunteers were refreshing. No one was ever injured during my watch. I kept a cooler full of water and ice, and plenty of snacks. I also kept a close watched on the welfare of the volunteers. The weather stayed hot and humid for the rest of the summer. I had a choice to spend sometime in the hotel where most of the company's employees were staying, but I elected to spend the whole time in a cargo camper.

The damage was impressive, on the east side of Calm Lake log cabins were ripped off their foundations; one was left in a dangerous lean. So many house were simply gone the debris was scattered all over the place. I saw a red pine plantation that was almost toppled over. There were many sad stories of loss. Still we worked to help get the job done and get people back living their lives.

Toward the middle of July part of the Siren crew was dispatched to Albert Lea. The Farmland Plant had been burning for two days our job would be to render the plant and prepare it for demolition. There were parts of the factory that fire fighters could not get to and the massive size of the building compounded with the fire's damage made parts of the fire inaccessible to fire fighters.

I was given a tour of the structure and the problems that the fire caused.

My first task was to help render out the loading dock.

The mess was a sight to see. Ankle deep in a moving blob of pigs fat and alive with maggots, the smell was overbearing. The problem was I was ready for it the rest of the crew wasn't. Our skid steer operator climbed out of the rig and threw up at my feet; I shovel the jelly like debris into the dumpster all of it so another smell wouldn't add to the mix.

By now most of the dock crew where getting sick to their stomach, I was moved to the basement to help with the pork bellies. I was told later that day after the one worker threw up by me and I had not reacted in a manner that the rest were not expecting they all got sick from my lack of reaction to what was happening around us.

In the basement though it was cooler by about 50 degrees, hanging racks of pork bellies and units of pressed or curing bellies waited for us, about 1 million pounds worth. In all over 3 million pounds of pork product was destroyed in the fire.

A conveyor was set up to help us remove the product into the bucket of a frontend loader that would when full transfer the debris to a roll-off dumpster or even a dump truck which ever was available at the time. The guys were complaining how this was not the work they were expecting in disaster mitigation, I just laughed at them. When they asked what was the worst I had to deal with I told about the body at Fort Sill that I had recovered, it had been in the woods for four months before anyone would find it. What was alive on that remains was very much what was alive on the loading dock floor.

Yes the smell was sickening however it wasn't as bad a learning that a 9 and 11 year old brothers exploring the wood and finding those human remains. The complaining stopped. Simple jokes would be shared and the job would become the punishment job for those who could misbehave themselves back in Siren. By the end of July both jobs were finishing up and FEMA would teach us about MASS Fatality Incident Management. Our briefing from FEMA started with **"Something very big is about to happen. We don't know when or where, it looks like it could involve airplanes and New York City. We pray the information is wrong but if something was to happen we need to get our response system ready. That includes this company as well."**

It was five week prior to 9/11 and this would be the second time I took one of these classes; the first time was after the 1993 attack on the World Trade Center. The following weekend I would go to my unit's annual training.

Once at annual training we were the combination of two different medical companies and a Forward Surgical Team (FST). It was difficult at first to get the pieces to work together our first day in the field got bogged down by the fact that this was the first time the FST trained in afield setting with their equipment and our doctrine wasn't set up to work with such an advance medical team, we were learning on the fly.

Once things got worked out we melted all the units together. The heat of the day started dropping some of the soldiers who were not good at watching their water consumption.

Back at Siren we had cases of emergency drinking water from Miller Beer; I had loaded some in the trucks before leaving for annual training and now broke the water out so that the troops can stay motivated to getting the camp set up. Everyone enjoyed the treat to the point even the company commander offered a bottle to our leadership when they passed through on a site inspection.

We did a site move and with the lessons learned from the first campsite, the second campsite was completely established in record time all facilities from the treatment tent, patient holding , the surgical tent and all the support sites and equipment to include the pharmacy truck was fully operational in under two hours. We were already seeing patients form the other units and started pulling MASCAL drills by night fall. First Sergeant took me out of the picture so that we could stand back and watch the soldiers work, they didn't need any leadership they could function without their platoon sergeant. I was also given word of a promotion to a medical platoon to a unit in northern Minnesota. This would be my last annual training with a unit I drilled with for over 13 years. The last day was hard to look back, but a lot was done.

When I first got the unit the Patient Hold Ward was the red headed step child of the company, unwanted by the platoon leadership and not desired by any of the enlisted. Now patient hold was a part of the team, no longer simply a sleeping tent put up for the fulfillment of army doctrine.

For one year I had my squad stationed at Camp Ripley as a detachment. There too it excelled on its own. At the same time I had came down with a ligament impingement in my right shoulder and went through the process to be medically boarded and excluded from push-ups for annual physical fitness testing. Still did sit-ups and two mile runs.

The explorer post and the out of the box training I had always put together to keep the training plan lively rather than to bog down into the repeated World War Two European training plan that was so over used from working with the DNR and the fires I had seen all the ways the guard help the communities. All I tried was prepare my guys to the best of my ability to have them just as ready for the civil call-ups as well as if the Russian marched across the German border.

I packed up my gear and move to the new unit. Kim and I took the drive to the new Armory. We were met by the Readiness NCO with **"What the ^@#%, you don't belong here."** The new unit was not going to accept the EPS promotion and I was instructed to return to my old unit rather than to push the issue. The new unit was hostile from day one.

I contacted my old unit to inform them what was happening. Once at drill I found a medical section that was in disarray. First thing was to do a complete inventory of equipment. The guys were not happy as both the Division Medical Supply Office representative and I broke into boxes of supplies that had been stashed and hidden in storage areas throughout the armory compound.

The boxes were part of a reconfigure that had occurred back in the early 1990's. Previous leadership just signed for the equipment and put everything else in storage without completing a shortage annex. The filing cabinet which should had held a training plan and records also stood empty.

11 SEPTEMBER 2001

I had just gotten home from a night of sweeping parking lots and had curled up to Kim and fell fast asleep, however the replaying of the second plane striking the World Trade Center woke me up. At first I thought it had to be a Cessna, not the large commercial jet that it was. My stirring woke Kim and she asked what was going on. I had simply told her that bin Laden just attack the World Trade Center again.

"Who" was her reply, and then the Pentagon was struck by the third plane.

It wasn't long and equipment was moving from Minnesota to New York, I had turned down my chance to go to New York since the platoon I inherited was in such a mess. The key problem turned out that I could not earn the respect of a junior NCO that held the momentum of the section. He did everything to the popularity of unit members and not the best interest of the unit.

Drills were the chance for the guys to go to the strip bars and play paint ball when ranges didn't have to be manned. Anything else that needed to be done was met by a **"Nope, negative we don't have to do that."**

Although I had been placed in a Sergeant First Class position the well connected junior NCO used his leverage to prevent the promotion. Even trying to go to Advance NCO Course for the unit was a fight. Still I was able to go to the first phase of ANCOC.

There was also the issue of the state healthcare workers strike that left many group homes without staff. Even though I cleared the background checks one of our lieutenants was a child protection worker from another county, after confining in him what I had gone through with county social services in the cities I was released from the assignment and sent home. Even though I had passed all background checks for a second review.

November 2001 I was sent to North Carolina for forest fire detail. Arriving to Ashville my driver and I had to have a fuel filter repaired on our truck before we could even sign in, it was leaking. As soon as we signed in we were sent to the Lamar Fire in Hot Springs. We spent three days working the fire and returned to Ashville for two days before being sent to the Winding Stairs Fire.

Topem, North Carolina was just around the bend of the road a short walk from the fire nothing more than a small store and mail drop. However as we worked the fire the FBI was always nearby. Eric Rudolph made his camp somewhere in the woods that our fire was burning in. The terrain was very rough and difficult to climb through much of the fire fighting would be done with helicopters since the ground was too unstable to send Hand crews in.

The instability was very well noted when we pulled up for the first night on the fire a hand crew from Porto Rico had a landslide run over the top of them as they attempted to cut a handline. The Appellation Mountains that made the up the topography of the fire area was simply high hills of loose rock cover with understory plants and trees sent their roots through the loose rocks. The plant life held everything in place when the plants brunt away and the trees fell over the rocks simply started shifting and rolling down hill.

On our first night we took position on one side of the line setting up a back burn to meet the advancing flame front. We had a good road to base off of and had reduced the briar brush along the road before we lit the back fire, with both met it was a light being turned off. Except for the top of the hill where the handline met the road. It was a sharp corner and we had worked the back fire to burn slowly around it and continue down slope.

The hope was by morning the fire could be slowed to a manageable level and the day crews would mop it up. However on the other part of the fire thing where not going well.

Both the fire and back fire combined and an aggressive wall of flames built momentum and got beyond the reach of the fire fighters. It lit the sky in a sunlight glow. We had to shift our position to assist. As we got to the top of the road were our other truck was it was surround by flames. Bang and thuds of rocks were heard has the landscape shifted sending debris to the road below. Going up the hill one of our rear dual tires got a rock up in between and the inner tire went flat.

We transfer what water we had into our other truck and put the remainder on the fire and went to the picnic site to change tires and refill with water from the creek below. By the time we had the tire changed and the water tank refilled we were instructed to return to our original assignment point on the fire.

The back fire work very well for this part of the line, much of the brunt area has cooled significantly in the cool morning air. Where we left the fire burning was slowly creeping and had advanced only a short distance in the two hours we were away from it and the fire was where we wanted it to be. The division supervisor and I took the handline down the hill while the driver met us below.

Little over halfway down the slope we discovered that the handline had not been completed, but it was in a drainage line that was wet from an artesian spring that kept the drainage bed filled with water. The fire above wasn't moving very fast, the day crew will be here within a half hour. With the morning dew aiding the slow movement of the fire the day crew will make quick work of tying in the final 1000 feet of handline to the valley below.

Like I said wildland fire fighting has to be more fire management verse suppression. The wilderness thrives on fire and needs occasional fire for the woods and grasslands to grow healthy. When it is possible and as well as safe to do so it is far better to let a section land burn rather than to put it out the fire. This section of the fire fit all the right criteria and a healthy burn was occurring.

The other section of the fire simply ran away from us; however there was a large space between the fire and any built up property. Still the land was impossible to access and the weather more than anything else stopped the fire.

We never found Eric Rudolph's camp as the FBI was hoping we would, however he would be caught 13 months later rummaging through the dumpster at the General Store just a quarter mile down the road from where this fire was.

Once back home I made up the guard drill I missed, but the unit remained a hostile work place and the leadership was hard to work with. Even though I had past positive experiences with the units leadership in the past this time nothing was working.

The company I had been working for had leased a building just down the street from my house. On the return from North Carolina though we saw spoils from New York City. Our general manager had pallets of bottle water and t-shirts drawn from the donations warehouse in New York and sent to back to Minnesota.

Some of the bottled water was being shipped to our crews working a training derailment in Minot, North Dakota. He was selling the water to another disaster contractor that requested our help.

The money the company was making helping with all these federal assignments was not good enough our manager wanted more. So for the amount of $93,000.00 in what he declared as excess stuff he set the company up for a criminal investigation and the lost in millions in federal fire support and suppression and disaster mitigation contracts.

For 2002 there would be no fire crews or work. I would have to wait until the investigation and trial process proves who was guilty and whose names are cleared from any wrong doings.

2002 started with the company denying all allegations against the company, this was the work of disgruntle worker and not management wrong doing. What made it bleak was when the FBI raided the company offices. Though for now we were allowed to work the words was getting out that we needed to think about our future and how to take care of our families.

By the end of February it wasn't looking real good for the company's future, but I had to go to ANCOC first before worrying about looking for a new job. A drive through Carlos Avery placed another worry. The water table was lower than when the fire burned through just 2 years prior the bottom of the peat bog was visible when I drove through.

Pat's actions and the investigation it caused would take 12 type 6 engines and over 300 fire fighters out of fire season. The thought of his greed sicken me.

At Fort McCoy our ANCOC instructor declared that **"If you're not willing to simply destroy another soldiers career then you didn't belong being sergeant first class."** We were encouraged to tell stories of our military career, but when I talked about the things I went through I was given a note by her calling me a lair and if anything I said was true then I should be a sergeant major by now. Back at the unit I found no support from my chain of command. I would not be seeing a promotion in the company.

By the end of March a wrong way driver would enter 35W southbound at County Road D. As the other drivers got out of the way I was cut off in the left hand line under the bridge. I had nowhere to go and clipped the car that had just cut me off. My little Ranger Pick-Up truck was totaled.

I started to look for another job. In the news Channel 5 caught a worker from the private adoption agency that I was referred to describe how their agency can legally hide a child from a father so the new born could be adopted without any legal recourse for him. Though the worker was shadowed out I recognized her by figure and voice that was someone I had originally talked to about my girls.

Later in the week the same news crew would catch a county social services Guardian ad-Latten claim their actions in support of the county and also claim; **"The only reason a father wants joint custody is because it is less money. It is not like a father really cares about his kids."** Was there a change in the wind? I really prayed for it however other problems were being dealt with.

The first issue came when my auto finance company billed for an additional $3,000.00 for the truck. By now they had been paid over $12,000.00 for a $10,000.00 loan. What we were finally informed about was the quick pay we used several payments were collected the day after the bill was due. The extra money demanded was a penalty for the late payment for their late processing of the bill, not based on the fact the payment was sent on time but not process until days later.

By now Kim were mainly wheelchair bound and the difficulties at work, the unit and now this. The world felt like it was closing in and the next hit was still coming.

An extended time period in between guard drills provide the opportunity to take drivers training through a trucking company in Salt Lake City. The promise was if we could maintain a year of employment with the company the training was free. Otherwise you had a choice; pay $1,800.00 or take out a $5,000.00 "Student Loan" from the company credit union.

I made through the classroom and was assigned to a trainer. Things were going well, I was slowly becoming comfortable with backing the 53 foot trailers behind the over the road tractors that were a studio apartment on wheels. My trainer was a Bosnian refugee who was in a lease purchasing contract for his tractor and looking forward to better times ahead as well.

With every dispatch of a load I reminded them of my upcoming guard drill, even put in for a military leave for the extended drill weekend that was coming up. When the travel day arrived the company refused to honor the military leave.

Instead I was sent from St. Louis, Missouri to Chicago, Illinois to pick up a trailer that was express loaded to Sacramento, California. There could be no route deviation no extra stops this load was to move the second it was released and not allowed anything but to arrive to its destination.

At 11pm Central Time the company told me that I was to be dropped off at the Greyhound Station in Chicago and catch a bus home, they were attempting to convince me to split train the drill for the companies benefit. They were not going to honor the leave request.

My trainer who was lease purchasing the tractor and realized this wasn't the agreement that was made earlier in the day with dispatch started to take me to St. Paul.

The GPS trackers kept the company aware of our location and threaten us with theft if we continued "Off Route". My trainer was not going to get in between the company and the U.S. Army. As we headed west without the trailer, I had my trainer drop me off at a truck stop in Beloit, Wisconsin. My hope was to either contact my relatives in Wisconsin or hitch a ride to get home for guard drill. His concern was if he owned the truck how could he be steeling his own tractor? We both express concerns about the honor of this company.

The company would fire me, my unit again failed to offer support and Department of Labor refused to enforce the law to the trucking company. In a three year period I had been ripped off by corporate greed by three different companies. I now owed in the companies word over $10.000.00 in disputed debts and no one to go to for support, not even the State Attorney General's office. Government agencies were not going to accept the word of the employee, just the word of the employer.

Position meant leverage, and being the employee meant you where not in the position of leverage.

By July I was released from my guard unit just months away from making the 20 year letter. Advised to go back to my old unit, but they wouldn't take me either. I drilled for three more months at that unit as I tried to find a new unit to go to. I was advised to get a copy of my records and the unit remained very hostile. IG wasn't any help either; I was basically on my own.

A buddy of mine was a recruiter when I turned the records over to him none of the allegation they used to release me where adding up, incomplete a vague counseling and the new unit I was now with was commanded by the wife of the previous Battalion Executive Officer.

She prepared for a **"Real dirt bag."** By the time annual training was completed she claimed that I was the issue of many household fights, she wanted to know what the old unit was actually doing. I was a far better soldier than what they tried to mislead me to be and was a self starter and had benefited the unit in more ways than ever expected.

There were a lot of problems with combat arm units in accepting the Enlisted Promotion System. It forced away developing a friend's career and work to develop all the talent that often overlooked and often exploited by some trying to climb the leadership chance. Individual stubbornness was used to block many careers from progressing. For now I saved my guard career.

Next was to search for the 20 year packet that the old unit hidden and was trying to keep from me. I had to call the state guard office in St. Paul to start the search. It was found in a fulltime staff member's desk back at the armory of the old unit and it was mailed to be prior to the window closing for its filing.

Since I was fired from the Salt Lake City trucking company I couldn't get unemployment so in September 2002 I was working for Andrew, a guard friend of my brother David who owned several trucks, two straight chaise van trucks and a day and line-haul tractor.

The trucks where getting old though, a previous partner had left his holding onto a $6,000.00. We sold our manufactured home to Anoka County for $3,000.00 and used some of that money to help another resident in the park repair her roof, staying for a short period until the double wide that was sold to us became available.

December 2002 our state senator had invited me to a hearing over changes purposed to the child support collections bill. The suggested change was to tailor the Minnesota system to more mimic the federal foster grant program. The plan if adopted would have required non-custodial parents to pay a minimum of $1,000.00 per child per month and if unable the non-custodial parent would be forced to surrender their parental rights.

The social experts claimed that this plan would be far more beneficial than the previous system that relied on a sliding scale based on actual income. With the large number of current child support in the rears many families were simply not being paid any support at all. The county was using those arrears to "Pay-Off" back child support services.

The biggest arguments to light was the fact that one, this plan was unreasonable at best, it was only designed to force the noncustodial parent to quit and surrender their parental rights knowing full well only a small percentage of non-custodial parents would ever afford the high cost of the purposed child support.

The second argument came from both child and parent alike, safe guarding visitation plans, since time with the child was more valuable than the money sent by the parent. A third argument stemmed for the misuse of child support funds for the outings of the mother rather than the needs of the child.

Too often a mother with a well paying job and a steep child support plan against the father was paying for her ski trips and spa outings no accountability was required for the child support fund.

By the time we could get the income to turn around the trucks started failing. However the bigger problem was military deployments had started pulling all of us to active duty.

I had spent a drill weekend training with the troops who were preparing to go to Bosnia acting as a civilian on the battlefield. As far as I knew any deployment for me would be a long way off.

I was the first to be sent to Kosovo for a 9 month deployment. Dana our other driver was deployed shortly afterwards to Iraq and Andrew would be deployed to Iraq right as I returned to Minnesota from my Kosovo trip.

IN THE WORST INTEREST

These pictures were taken during the 1996 Spring Fire response.

The above picture; Taken at the assembly at the Duluth, Minnesota National Guard Armory near the Duluth Airport.

Upper right picture; Taken at one of the many drop points that was around the fire.

Center picture: Taken as we climb up the slope near a river and led to a power line clearing in the Boulder Creek Wilderness, Oregon.

Bottom picture: Taken as our Crew Boss rested prior to the hike out for the end of the day.

JAM

2000 Eastern Idaho Fire Severity Staging. Top picture was our line up in a park in Idaho Falls.
The next two here working a burnout line to another fire that I have long forgot the name.
The crew ahead of us had been setting the back fire we back off and patrolled the line.

The bottom pictures the images are closer than they appear. I could feel the heat through the window glass

These picture where taken on an old fire that during a weather change had rekindled

These pictures were taken during the Carlos Edge Fire in the Carlos Avery Wilderness Area near Forest Lake, Minnesota. In the bottom picture I am holding some of the foam that was coming out of our. Butch Murphy was my driver and the young lady was from the water tender that was supplying the water to the many trucks that was working the fire. Within an hour of this picture I would get my right hand burned as I tried to get the gas can to refill the pumps tank.

The helicopter was from the Minnesota Army National Guard and would be from the unit I would spend my second tour to Iraq with.

Pictures from the response to the Winding Stairs Fire near Topem, North Carolina.

Above picture was taken during our weekend in Regensburg Germany.

The upper right was taken on a Sunday at Camp Bondsteel; note I do have a pistol on my hip.

The bottom picture is of the pedestrian gate of Camp Montieth where my unit was stationed while in Kosovo.

At the front gate of the KFOR base in Pristina, Kosovo

Evening at Camp Bondsteel with Big Duke the distance.

Two helicopters taking off from Camp Montieth. Giljaine Kosovo in the background

At the first aid skills tent for Expert Infantry Badge testing at Camp Bondsteel.

Sitting in a door gunners seat waiting for takeoff

In one of the rooms we lived in while in Kosovo

The top picture was assisting with the Expert Infantry badge 12 mile road march. This was the second attempt and I was held at a fixed point and not allowed to repeat the road march.

Bottom picture 1LT H. and I are taking a break from zone patrols just days after the rioting, the Bradley Infantry Vehicle was one of the units that was part of the rapid repair of the units that were left at the base a neglected prior to our arrival

Yes I did spend a little time playing a Game Boy however it wasn't that often.

Sundays meant we could wear civilian clothing, however we had to always carry our side arms.

On a sign port in Camp Bondsteel was an omen of things to come.

Family pictures of Mischief and I relaxing at home and Kim's oldest boy Jimmy below

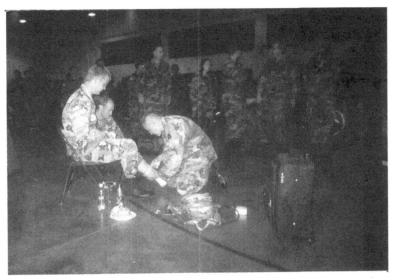

Getting ready for my first trip to Iraq had me playing Medic as another soldier sprained his ankle on the day we formed up to leave.

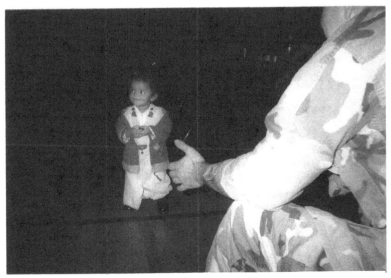

Jen's daughter Kendra surprised all of us by taking her first real steps and discover that she could walk around the armory.

Final pictures before the bus would take us to the airport. My mom, Jen and her kids and my wife Kim with final hugs before it was time to go.

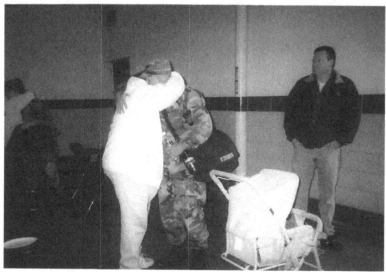

In the bottom picture our church friend Todd watched as Kim and I had our final hug before I climbed on the bus.

IN THE WORST INTEREST

Top picture was one of the last pictures of my girls that I would ever take. We had stopped at a playground prior to taking them back to the foster home. In court their foster mother would claim that they were covered in mud and the littlest one was sick.

Middle picture is of Kim as she endured radiation therapy for throat cancer. It was a hard decision to take the second trip, but with the collapse of the banking industry it turned out to be the wisest one made.

Bottom picture was taken of me coming home from my first tour to Iraq.

171

KFOR 5B

David was slowly preparing for a medical discharge when his unit was alerted alerted for the deployment. This unit both Andrew and Dana belong to, but none of the three would go. The unit needed a lead medic. So on a day in late August 2003 while I was making deliveries my work cell phone began to ring. By the end of the day I was going on active duty in less than a week. This unit was also the unit of my daughters adopted brother, but he had transferred out and then to the air guard right I was assigned for this mission.

Initially the squad had, a junior NCO, a PFC medic and two female medics one E-4 (Specialist) with me being the squad leader and unit senior medic. We would gain two additional medics once we left the training site and started out mission. Training would involve three months at Fort Steward, Georgia and 1 month Germany before spending 6 months in Kosovo. At the end would be close to one month of terminal leave spend your last days of active duty enjoying some well deserved time off.

Right before my departure on the deployment David moved into the house needing a place to live, while there we had three other friends staying with us briefly. However those friends were asked to leave because of problems they brought with them and how those problems were affecting us.

David would later move to mom's having his medical situation was becoming far more difficult than Kim could manage. One of the problems David was dealing with was a burning anger, though never violent his expressions hinted to the affects of my first wife abuse of him so many years before.

Whatever exchange between my daughters adopted brother and David at guard drills I would never know, however it may have never helped with the plight of this long term separation from my daughters and may have encouraged the transfer to the air guard for him and lengthen the separation between my daughters and I.

For now it was train for war. While at Fort Steward I learned that setting up for Combat Life Saver training by a medical section for a unit was far simpler than what was led to believe by the old guard unit. I had within a week set up training for our infantry men to be able to take care of themselves during security patrols. Too often patrols would have to be conducted without a medic since there would be no room in the vehicles of the patrol for the extra personnel. Our guys needed to be proficient.

Even though we were on active duty status our medical leadership refused to give permission to conduct training on intravenous injections, stating it wasn't allowed by their state medical command to view as too risky of training to conduct. We trained anyways and were finally supported by higher command and vital training for the mission.

Later on we were conducting all the training for our task force and throughout the deployment we provided the medical skills training.

The days were filled with training and equipment issue for individual, section and unit. An opportunity to renew my Emergency Medical Technician rating was available but was turned down by the task force command; we would accomplish the required training during the actual mission than during the train up period.

The 3rd Infantry Division was returning from Iraq and battle damaged equipment lined the railhead into the base. Other guard and reserve units were reporting in for their Operation Iraqi Freedom deployments and the base was a hub of activity.

One thing making the news while we were at Fort Steward was the treatment of wounded soldiers. All of our billets where fairly run down brick buildings set up as bays for 60 individuals on bunk beds. The ceilings were not insulated and open to the rafters a garage heater was the furnace for chilly nights and the only form of air conditioning was by keeping the windows open and fans on.

With the bay filled with soldiers' body heat and respirations made the air heavy and stifling. Our bathroom was a separate building outside. Many of the builds cracks in the mortar let sunlight shine through the wall rather than just the windows. Most days were simply a humid 80 to 90 degree haze. But as Christmas approached the nights got very cold.

When word got out that severely wounded soldiers were in the same living conditions as the soldiers training to go to war it just didn't look right. A person with a leg missing expected to get on and off the top bunk was a just not realistic and other problem were address by the investigation. This was simply a distraction on our way over there.

During some off time we all got to go to Savannah, Georgia I made a pen pal who wrote throughout the trip as well as during the next two deployments to come. Laura had given her kids up to her husband thinking that by making him be the parent he would fail and she could then maintain sole custody without having to deal with the issues the counties services would cause.

She guessed wrong, he turned out to be a very good father and very able to raise the kids. She regretted using her kids in the manner she did. However she did take care of the child support and maintain her visits and as the kids got older a better relationship with them grew.

She helped try to send a box of gifts from Kosovo to my daughters which were rejected and sent back to her. I had tried to mail a small box of Christmas presents before I had left to go overseas on my own only to find out they too were rejected and sent to the dead letter pile.

We had a week off for the holidays and got to go home before the flight overseas.

The first flight to take off had our task force leadership on; we were on a later flight. The air force were flying us in C141 jets that were on their last flights before being sent to the bone yard and phased out of the air force inventory. Several planes broke down in flight and required repairs to continue with the mission. Our plane was no exception. We had a day delay for repairs.

Once in Germany we discovered that the flight with the leadership was still delayed due to repairs. Their plane would break down a second time in flight and their delay was over a week after we arrived to the training base. When we arrived to the campsite I was standing on a familiar hill. I had been on that same patch of ground 21 years prior.

There was the building we took the written exam for the Expert Field Medical Badge. The open field across the street that we camped in and the road we took the 12 mile road march on. I was standing on the very spot where in July 1983 I earned that training badge for my uniform signifying that I was one of the best military medics in the army.

Now the site is set up as a mock forward base with weather worn tents that were impossible to keep heat in and ours was missing it's zippers in the corners. For the most part we just provided medical support while the rest of the task force trained for the mission. My one sergeant was showing to be quite a problem; his dad had rank in his home guard command so he tried to get away with everything he could.

Our first Sunday in country our unit arranged a bus to tour

the City of Regensburg. We spent the whole day there first touring the Natural History Museum, then the Dome of St. Peter and finally to some German and Irish pubs there. There we found and meat shop with the family name on it and had a very enjoyable time. This trip the German folks were very hospitable none of the expressions I had witnessed on the last tour to Germany were ever seen.

People, some who may have protested the American bases twenty years ago were now greeting us with open arms and pints of German Lager. Some places it was like meeting up with good friends. It was refreshing to see Germany again.

At the end of the months training we had one final chance to see the Germany country side. I had chosen to walk to the village that bares the camp name. Back at the camp my two sergeants were planning their next move. Having gotten into trouble by sneaking off on another trip they had drawn 24 hour watch for the treatment tent.

They were relieved in the morning and had planned their own one day trip. However they got divided and one found his own way to Regensburg and since he didn't know how to read German became stuck overnight with no way back to camp.

His equipment wasn't even packed for the next days' flight and he showed up missing movement and the Command Sergeant Major packed his bags finding 3 bottles of wine hidden in his luggage. He was reduced to the rank of Specialist on the spot.

My squad had already been reassigned with a new sergeant when a medical was blown on his watch. He wasn't comfortable conducting the duties as a medic; he was a medic because it was something easy for him to do.

His situation was a headache for much other the tour. My other sergeant was constantly using his connection to help the relieved sergeant his rank back through all sorts of different schemes. None of them worked.

We settled into camp and the place called Kosovo.

We provide a mix of services, combined troop medical clinic, base ambulance and company level support. Our base was an old Yugoslav army base located in the city of Gjilane. A grain elevator had the full view of the camp and would have made a great snipers nest if anyone desired. For the most part the tour was very peaceful and we were collecting combat pay.

March 12th and our task force was fully in charge, within days the last of the unit we relieved had returned to home. Camp Montieth was our own along with contractors from KBR and ITT Security Forces. Our living arrangement was a building that had 6 bays as living units. One of the six was set up as the latrine and shower but he rest could house up to 20 per bay. We had four of us sleeping in one bay. We had also picked up a medic from Alaska for our squad.

March 17th was a Sunday and it was a warm comfortable day. Sundays were the day that if you did not have any duties you could be in civilian clothes. I had just turned a load of dirty laundry to the laundry point and then went to Camp Bondsteel and checked out the Post Exchange there. An hourly bus traveled between the camps all day long.

However on my return things were not looking right in the country side. Massive amount of people were gathering together in all the little towns between the two camps. One last bus would make out of camp Bondsteel before all the camps in Kosovo locked down. Once I arrived back to camp I quickly changed into uniform and went to find out what was going on.

The story went that on Thursday March 14th a criminal execution had occurred leaving one person of Serbia decent dead in a field. Saturday two boys of Albanian decent drowned in a stream in Mitrovita and the claim was they were chased by Serbians retaliating for the death on Thursday. By Sunday evening the clash of rioting could be heard everywhere. I had a front row view from the patio of the troop medical clinic as homes and cars burned. We prepared for a mass amount of injuries. However several of our medics were still trapped at camp Bondsteel unable to return.

JAM

Then the story of Abu Ghraib Prison in Iraq broke.

Luckily what was happening in Iraq was not adding to our problems. Three hairy days of rioting was all it wrote, but after 22 killed and over 600 injured the story in Kosovo turned out to be false, the oldest brother had made the story up when his two younger brothers drowns as he let them go swimming in the cold mountain stream.

For those three days though, it was intense. First my "B" team from Kamanica arrived needing to resupply and set up a forward medical station in the forward camp. We drew enough supplies to set up a small aid station and I went there with them to set it up.

The rest of my squad was accounted for and the forward team needed the extra help there. My goal was to go there and assess the full need. The "A" team was on the overnight ambulance duty for the week and their shift were well set up headed by a capable team leader.

The next day was a long day each of the medics at the forward base went out on patrols. However the specialist of the group had been calling back to the TMC begging to be relieved he didn't want to be there. The night before was very close for those two.

A local elderly Serbian male had his car flipped while he was in it then drugged out of his car and severely beaten with a hammer. Though he lived the wounds were debilitating. Our patrol that was there had to transport the injured man to the Serbian boarder since the local clinic refused to treat him fearing that would bring the rioters to their door.

Still the treatment room was set and I was housed with the platoon leadership, the other two medics shared their own room. Later I was moved into the treatment room. It wasn't that I was there for long.

The "A" team leader took on himself to relieve the other team leader and the specialist, I returned to camp to find an uproar caused by my team leaders' departure, he had abandoned his shift so he could get into the fight and brought one of the female medics with to stir the pot.

On the way back to Camp Montieth the logistics convoy had to driver through a line of rioters. I was riding in a canvas sided HMMWV with our First Sergeant driving, my pistol drawn and ready to fire if anyone touched the door. I prayed heavily that we would pass without a problem.

Our family history since the First World War has been severed without firing a single shot, this was not the day I wanted to break tradition, and relief was driving through the camp gate with the same rounds that I started the day with.

The next problem was the unit was reading to respond to Mitrovita, the Greeks had lost control and were pushed out of the city. When we took over the camp only a couple of the Bradley Infantry Fighting Vehicles were mission ready, most had been severely neglected with rusting weapon systems and tracks with more pads worn than required to drive on city streets or just plain broken down.

The maintenance teams and gun crews worked over night to get things right. I drew an ambulance and set up another stash of medical supplies to go out on the extended mission we were preparing for. We also pooled extra resources were we could.

The biggest problem I was facing was with my team leaders. The "A" team leader was requested by our company commander to accompany the unit on this mission. He was in fact assigned to the company and the other companies in this task force were able to recall their assigned medics for the increased mission support.

However the "B" team leader was on his week with the company and didn't want to be stuck with the ambulance detail. Both team leaders pressed their respective higher leadership to influence the decision into their personal favor. I had sat them down and waited until someone would finally back down and we could get the focus on the mission.

We had the time to do this since movement was on an indefinite hold while the actual mission need was reassessed.

Meanwhile parts of the infantry battalion that were stationed in Bosnia had been flown to Camp Bondsteel and already to make the move northward as well. That move never happened, once the word got out that the riots were over a false tale people quickly returned home. The following weekend the school children had a protest for peace. Things quieted down very quickly.

With the rioting stopped the clean up begun. Word of the lie traveled as fast as the call to riot. Civil representatives could only hang their heads; this riot was a huge waste of time, life and property. The relationship that had been built with the American forces had been insulted by their country men's actions; we had a lot of work to do.

First was to motivate the people to clean up their mess. As a third world country it was in the typical mess. For years creek beds became landfills in hope that the spring melt and rain would wash the debris downstream and out of sight, out of mind. During the riots through trash was thrown everywhere. The streets were the first to be cleaned.

A proposal was presented to train the Kamanica Fire department a watered down version of the army's Combat Life Saver Course. The patrols discovered that the fire department was both under trained as well as under equip for the support of the community. We couldn't do anything about the lack of equipment, but training was up our alley. We pulled out the portions of the course that would not have any real benefit for the fire department and gave the rest.

At first the medical leadership refused to support this project, but both our company commander and the squad express an interest to provide the training. The "A" team leader made it happen while I spent the first month in Camp Bondsteel as part of the first rotation to conduct the army medic transitions training that we didn't do during train up.

We had the class material into translated both Serbian and Albanian language and each week squad members had conducted the class. By now only one person stayed at the forward base to provide medical support. Also stationed there was a small detail of military police and civil affairs. My medics worked well with all of them.

On the weekend I was to report to Camp Bondsteel for the medic transitions course a Jordan Police Officer hired by the United Nations fired his pistol at the American police officers that they were sharing assignment at the Provencal Prison. Another person was dead and a female American police officer lay in an intensive care bed at the camp hospital.

The medic training included the full Emergency Medical Technicians course and advance skills such as advance airways including endrotracheal tubes and needle chest decompression, a skill used to treat a traumatic condition call a tension pneumothorax which is air leaking around an injured lung and fills the chest cavity with pressurized air as the patient slowly becomes unable to breath. Something I got to witness over 20 years prior when two soldiers had a serious accident back at Fort Sill.

Skills testing became another part of the deployment with the Expert Infantry badge testing for the two infantry units that were part of the overall deployment, the other was assigned to Camp Bondsteel. The medics had to assist with the 12 mile road march.

The 6 mile hike left the camp and went down a road that was to the east of the base. It was beautiful countryside once we left the city area. I had assigned one medic to the three mile mark and to with the ambulance at the turn around point. I walked with the walkers make sure to check on everyone I came to along the way. All the stops had me across the finish line in 3 and a half hour, I had past the platoon sergeants along the way. They repeated the march and assigned me to a post I wasn't going to walk another. I had out walked an infantry company.

European cities are very different than American mainly because they build upwards and most property are not based around a large lot. The common yard had the street facing building that would often have a family business on the street level, be it a shop, a store, a pub. Then there would be at least three stories of apartment above the family business. Through the gate would lead to a courtyard that would have the barn and, or more housing.

The city maybe a small dot on the map but in a community that held over 30,000 it was less than 2 miles wide and 4 miles long with plenty of farm field in between each town. Kamanica was the same way, yet it was less than a mile wide and two miles long and had over 10,000 in population. The dedication was to preserve the farm land. Farmers brought the hay to the cows in the barns or herded them out to graze in the fields. A small tractor that could tow a trailer or be converted into a tiller machine was the main farm implement. Few communities had larger tractors that was shared among the farms, but every farmer had the small one eye machines

At Camp Bondsteel heat injuries took out several hikers and put one in serious condition in the hospital. We had none on either walk. During the skills testing phase I ran the first aid skills station.

Back at Camp Montieth we did training with the units Combat Life Savers and I did CPR classes since I was able to get instructor training back at Fort Steward before we left,

Now I was using it regularly to help both the soldiers and the fire fighters in Kamanica.

For the squad of medics we kept ourselves busy and the six month deployment went by very quickly.

Near the end of the deployment of task force which was lead by a cavalry unit conducted a Spur Ride. This was where candidates would test in a variety of different military skills. There was at least 6 of the medics would to try my A Team Leader gave up after the PT portion of the morning. We conducted PT with our body armor on for about 45 minutes. Then we had a written test and two different sets of hands-on skills. The last set was conducted at night and along the same route as the 12 mile road march.

The day lasted for 36 hours by the time I went to bed and I

missed a chance to video conference home. My feet were sore and I actually felt good with all the physical activity. A group of restaurants had sent steak over and we had a great steak dinner that night. Going home was just around the corner.

First an interpreter invited me to meet his family in Pristina. The work we did with fire department was recognized not only by the unit, but civil affairs and the interpreters as well. He wanted a chance to show appreciation for the hard work. It a great home meal and a chance to see up front how life really was in Kosovo.

The squad of medics I led was the squad of action, we did more and time flew by. There were many accomplishments. The life saving action of the two medics during the riot, the training of the fire department, and keeping the Combat Life Saver skills on task served the task force well. We had also been assigned the task of working medical coverage for the APOD (aerial port of departure) which was shared by another squad and it last only for a couple of weeks until taken over by closer medical assets. The other squad had dump their ambulance in a ditch when another driver heading head on in a risky pass forced them into the ditch. Only the mirror was damaged and the two medics escape without injuries.

I had been approached by one of the other company commanders claiming he was disappointed that his medics didn't even try to stay in contact with company. He never knew who his medics were. All in all it was a great deployment and the new unit was arriving and training into the job, we were packed consolidated into fewer housing units and on cots rather than beds waiting to go home.

The flight was delayed because another plane broke down. It took two attempts to get out of Kosovo. As we arrived to the airport in Pristina the broken plane waited at the end of the taxiway, another plane was coming for us, it just wasn't there yet.

Once we took off nearing sunset we flew to Fort McCoy, Wisconsin for demobilization it was a very quick process in within a few days was back home in Minnesota and reunited with our families. Still it would be 3 months before I was back to the unit. First problem was I had no job to come home to.

Andrew was preparing to leave for his mobilization training station and reviewing all the needs with Dana gone I would not be able to effectively run his trucking business with him gone. I would look for another job while he was away and wait for his return. I went back to driving a bus.

God must been trying to talk to me for it seemed like at least once a month somewhere I was coming up to an accident. The first accident was within three blocks from our house. It had been a rough week. During the day I was training at the bus company and coming home tried from long drives across the state as we all learned to drive a couch bus.

Monday night I came home to find Kim on her scooter at the strip mall across the street from our house. The fire department had their truck on the far side of the parking lot and things did not look right. I went over to the store to meet my wife and one of the store managers stopped me.

"Hey John, Isn't the proper practice for a report of a gas leak to evacuate the whole building?" The fire department had cordoned off the vacant store and one of the fire fighters was holding the door open with his butt, smoking a cigarette. Thursday I went to the city council meeting to address my concerns. Friday night I was preparing to make my first orientation trip for the bus company to Kansas City when Kim and I left to go to our friend Lynn's house to help set up a birthday party for her son Josh.

A gentleman had left the local bar after drinking since noon. There was a light rain in the air, the street light at the intersection was out and he was wearing dark clothes. The best I could tell he was dead before he landed on the pavement. The young lady driving never had the chance to see the victim; her windshield was draped over the steering wheel and into her lap.

The local newspaper ran a story idolizing him as a town

hero for buying drinks for the fire department and having his own table at the bar. We stopped giving press releases for my deployments because some kids and one of the fire fighters would harass Kim while I was on deployment. A month later I was told to stop complaining about the fire department by the city attorney. Regardless of the amount of emergency services training certificates, the city doesn't honor them as valid and I wasn't needed for the fire department or the community.

This time it was an overnight route between either Minneapolis to Kansas City, Madison, Fargo or Sioux Falls. Eventually I would settle for a Duluth run that had me home each night and paid pretty good, but just not enough to pay all the bills. While I ran the Sioux Falls run the other bus on the route was highjack by a knife wielding female passenger. The bus was stopped by a stop stick and the driver was slashed in the attacked. Kim had been with me for the trip and once we got home phone messages were waiting for us, family worried if the victim was me. After the attack by my first wife I don't think I could had handled the situation as well as Ron did.

6 weeks after the gas leak at the strip mall a building in Ramsey, Minnesota would explode from a gas leak caused by a faulty connector. Because the gas had seeped through over 6 feet of dirt the odorant had been filtered out and the occupants were unaware of the problem until it was too late.

Everyone in the building was killed. A review of the counties gas pipeline system discovered the strip mall and our manufacture housing park all had the same faulty connector on the pipes. Emergency repairs were in order.

By May I may had stopped at over 8 different accidents as one of the first EMT's on the scene, contacting 911 and giving a scene report so the right equipment would be put en route and care and comfort to any of the injuries until the ambulance arrived. Just trying to be a helpful John Q. Public and use my skills for someone in need benefit.

The last car accident that I stopped at during this time occurred in May shortly before learning of my acceptance to the Fish and Wildlife fire crew. Kim had gone through gastric bypass surgery, and had been recovering very well. We were taking a friend of her home. For some reason I felt the need to take Minnesota 70 west of Rush City when up ahead the cars came to a complete stop. **"What?"** Kim asked **"Can you smell these accidents?"**

There was a black Saturn on its side in the ditch. I got out of the car to see if I could help. There under carriage was facing toward the direction I had parked the car, as I came around the car to see the butt of the victim pointing up and a very upset lady on her cell phone to 911. While his backside was up outside of the car the top of the car was pushing down on his stomach just above the belly button; he was resting on the rear passenger door facing up.

I took checked his pulse and he started to come to. The car was too unstable to enter. I relayed all the information to the 911 operator and check the scene of any additional victims. There were none to be found and soon the ambulance and fire department would arrive it was a great sound to hear him screaming in pain, at least he was alive and Kim would have to sit through another fatality accident waiting for me to be cleared by the investigators.

We had often talked about my plans to of developing into a fire suppression and support services contractor, but never really had the resources. Still I longed to be back on the fire lines and doing the services that by know I really believe was my calling from God. Many of the hard lumps I was taking seemed to verify the calling rather than to discourage from pursuing it.

Summer was coming. Route bids were also coming up and I would lose my route that turned around at the University of Minnesota Duluth Campus.

One day on while I was on the Duluth route my bus broke down in Rush City and it would take nearly three hours before we got on our way again. I had all the telephone numbers that I needed to get the students to the downtown bus terminal to catch the actual Greyhound and had nearly an empty bus on my return.

Then another day a picked up a gentleman who was heading for the Amtrack station, with him was the familiar red pack of a forest fire fighter. I too had been bidding for a slot and so far had not been selected by any agencies. I was giving up and started looking at a truck driver job with the post office when the FedEx came announcing the selection to the Charles M. Russell National Wildlife Refuge, I was back on the truck.

One of the delays in the selection was the fact anyone with ties to the disaster company were on hold until the criminal conviction came indicating who was and wasn't guilty of fraud. Once satisfied that the guilty where in fact behind bars the rest of us could have our lives back. May 31st 2005 I was heading west to a small town called Jordan, Montana.

Another factor that led me to this route of fire services was to the fact that a metro area fire chief apparently lobbied to the governor of Minnesota to disband the DNR call when needed fire roster. From what I had learned this metro fire chief felt it was an unreliable list since fire fighters that had been forced off local community fire departments were finding a second chance of the list. He didn't feel that dishonored fire fighters deserved a second chance by anyone.

Given his attempt was to remove a full 400 man roster to retaliate against one fire fighter, his efforts only changed the program, the targeted individual remained in fire fighting.

WILDFIRES AND T-REX BONES

It was a long drive and after a short stop at a friend's house in Steele, North Dakota for supper. I arrived to the Jordan Field Office. It was about 4 am and I was very tried. I woke up to car doors closing I met my supervisors. I needed to continue driving to Lewistown and get my paperwork done. 120 more miles left in the trip, but I was able to unpack first and was assigned the service truck to finish the trip.

I felt like for the time in my adult life I had finally came home.

Some of the residents of Jordan had hard feelings of government employees since this was the area of the Freeman Standoff in 2000, but I was there to be a fire fighter, there to protect them. Some I shared my story with them, I too had reasons to mistrust how any given government agency works, however I know it is the choice individual workers make rather than policy that causes the issues. Though I as much of any man I am able to stubble, fall, trip or fail. I have always desired to service my community first. Even such I am writing for the encouragement of my grandchildren not for any glory or accolades of man. Serve from the heart.

The bunkhouse was comfortable and I could call home every

night. With plenty of calling cards from the deployment with me I would not be creating any phone bills.

Guard drills other than annual training was split trained in Montana with a field artillery unit that had armories in Glasgow and Malta. I was actually making friends.

We had one small fire before I had to return to Minnesota for National Guard Annual training. Even that was one of the best training periods in a long time. I had proven that every unit needs a medical section. I was constantly support or assisting with someone's training. While coming home from Montana I was nearly sideswiped by a Mail truck that had gotten confused and was taking the wrong lane from St. Cloud to Minneapolis.

All I could see was the trailers tire rack getting with inches of my car and my horn was not working.

When annual training was over with I had a little over a day with Kim before heading back to Montana. I was feeling my best and was happy to pull back into the field station for the rest of the summer. Fourth of July was around the corner and the VFW invited all veterans to ride or walk along side their float. Fireworks were launched over the bunkhouse by the fire department. By July I had been accepted to be on the county ambulance crew.

An accident had killed a popular local boy and the regular volunteers needed someone else to share the calling for the community. I was issued a county emergency radio and charger and set it by the bed.

For the up and coming first or second season fire fighters Jordan can be too quiet of a station. Though large fires had happened in the refuge they were far and few compared to other offices and the hotshot crews. For an old fire horse it was perfect. I had some fires and ambulance calls as well. I was used to 1000 calls per year. Thus summer 2005 eight fires and eight medicals was the perfect pace. It was enough to allow me feel reconnected to myself and I went home with accomplishment, and a Buck Knife gift to prove it.

For the most part the fires we had were small the largest at initial attack grew to 900 acres and was named the Macalester Fire. The largest fire that we conducted a patrol on was 13,000 acres but the fires name escapes me.

For the most part when dispatched for a fire to the refuge it was a long drive. Some areas it would take almost three hours to get there. Most of the roads travelling over 50 mph would be an unsafe speed and even 30 mph would make the travel treacherous. No good wrecking the truck and never getting to the fire. So off we went the smoke column visible in the distance and it always seemed to take eternity to get there.

You would think that by the time we would arrive the fire should be 1000 acres or larger, but the first fire wasn't even 2 acres in size, if that. The Dirka Fire was in the Lost Creek drainage skunking around in vegetation that had deep roots that reached into the shallow water table. A lighting strike fire that could not get going there was too much water in the plant life there.

Much of the fire was on a steep slope that led to a trail, a natural fire break that it didn't have the momentum to cross a quick handline and 600 gallons of water later morning came to show this fire was cold out and would not be an issue for the rest of the summer.

A week later rehab of the area and the fire was declared out.

It was the Macalester Fire that would make the news and have the heaviest activity of all the fires we fought for the summer. This fire bordered some private grazing land to the south and the Missouri River to the north, but weather forecasted erratic winds the following day in the mid afternoon. We tried a burnout the night before nut the back fire wouldn't build momentum during the night. In the morning the back burn area was almost out only in the lower valley was it burning. The crews spent the morning trying to make the line more secure.

Shortly after lunch signs of the impending problems where already showing. In the last effort to secure the line the weather was getting hotter and drier. The wind started its shift and a heavy smoke started building, this fire was getting ready to run. We pulled our hose lines right when the order came to evacuate the line. The trucks cleared the fire area and parked to the south east of the fire as a strong northeasterly wind brought the fire to life. Cut off from us was the Fork Peck Native American Crew that took shelter with their bus at the rivers bank north of the fire.

I had seen this before with the grassfires in my high school years; rivers had a huge effect on fire behavior. The cooler water would cause turbulence the wind and the rivers banks would channel and redirect the winds in all sorts of actions and directions. The fire began to roar.

As everyone watched I climb on the tool box of the truck and took a short nap tonight would be long one. However the fire slowed down in the grazed land. The grass was too short to carry the flames far. In deep valley were the cattle had not gotten deep into still burned but over the top of the hills and drainages were not enough plant life to keep the fire momentum. That night at supper a sick fire fighter was brought to me for a quick evaluation. I told him to take it easy for the next day.

The next day was a long one. All day we worked the areas were the fire hit the hardest. Other hand crews were coming in to finish the job so the engines can return to initial attack mode and be ready for the next fire. However the fire fighter that was sick the night before was working as hard as ever and by supper I had to take him to the hospital and would be off the line over night. It would take three hours to get to Lewistown form the fire.

First it was the attempt in the dark to find the main highway. As long as I headed for the street lights I would hit pavement, except I would take a wrong turn and started heading away from the lights. It was only about fifteen minutes before I realized my error but it was still lost time. By 1 am we pulled up to the emergency room. The fire fighter was suffering from the early stages of heat exhaustion and would require over three bags of fluids to rehydrate.

The policies of B.I.A. required that we break for eight hours before heading back to the fire so dispatch set us up in a hotel for the night near the hospital. In the morning after a breakfast we went to the field office and made sure the paperwork was square before returning to the fire. Unfortunately one of the crew members had a family emergency and we had to stop and call dispatch to get the information. I didn't get back to the fire until 2pm.

With the drive back to Jordan another three hours added to the trip and the work day the bed felt great.

In the Jordan Field Office hangs the plaster cast of a T-rex skull found in the Hell Creek area of the refuge. Turns out there have been many dinosaur finds in the area and Tim had shown me what a bone pile looks like form one that had been recently uncovered.

In between fires the fire crew did project work. Change a fence line for a cattle crossing to keep herds out of the refuge was a big task. Where the fence line crossed the road into Hell Creek it was at a spot that would encourage severe erosion first plan was to adjust the fence line to accommodate a location that would cause the erosion.

The next task was an exotic plant abatement project. This project actually had a travelling team of experts working the issue to help return the refuge into a more natural pre-1800 ground cover of plants. Fires help with some, but to allow unwanted plants in one area would spread into the areas that burned and a viscous cycle would begin. Our task was to try to break the cycle with damaging the other plants and wildlife.

We also handcrafted road signs with a router and 2x8" boards. The signs were simple and probably save the taxpayer a hefty sum of money and it was fun to work together with. The rustic signs just seem to fit the refuge appeal. By late August the bow hunters would come to hunt elk. There were large herds all over the place and while working fires we often woke to the sounds of bull elk calling. A good sign that the fire was almost out would be witnessed when a bull elk entered one of the fire areas and watched us s we worked.

A fire dispatch to Snow Creek was another fire. The county fire department had been working the fire for most of the day. We had missed the dispatch; it had not been announced over our radio frequency. When we got there much of the fire was out except for the fires rear which was backing into the wind in a way I have never seen before. The flame front was over 6 feet in height and burn vigorously, like it was actually the front of the fire.

Both the wind and the hills slope were against the fire it was the fine dry grasses that was feeding the fire. What we should have seen was a slowly backing fire going downhill and against the wind. Two airplanes circled and set up for the fire retardant drop. The airplanes were called Air Tractors, commonly used for crop dusting and easily converted for forest fire attack plane. Both carried about 800 gallons of the red stuff and they would drop their payload in a line to slow the fast advancing rear of the fire before it could cross into the creek bed.

The first plane came in so low it was about 6 feet off the ground and opened his payload door, it was a beautiful line just prefect and were it was needed the flames under the line of retardant was now pocket of smoldering embers. The next plane set up his approach, the plane lost lift and nearly hit the ground when the pilot gunned the plane and rapidly climb dropping his payload at the same time. This time there was no spread just a ball of liquid dropping to the ground into a small area never hitting the active flames. The flame front though was reduced and we could tie the fire line together and put out any remaining hot spots.

One of the county fire fighters got sick in the heat and I escorted him back to the vehicles. I took my time to make sure he was ok and recovering before I returned to the line. The BLM and refuge fire fighters would spend the night while the county fire fighters went home. In the morning there were only a few hot spots left, we had them out before noon and returned to our base in before the sunset. For the summer of 2005 Montana had fires all over the place, our little office still only had small fires compared to the other offices and agencies that we would work with.

August came to a close as much of the crews started to leave for college. The last service project as a whole crew was to help build hangers at each office site for the law enforcement air plane. We built the hanger at the Jordan Air Port. Word from the Minnesota Army National Guard was for a large deployment of troops to Iraq. My name was bouncing on and off the list.

September 29th and the fire season for me was finally done. The trucks were winterized and parked into the carports and the bunkhouse cleaned. The night before leaving we had on last ambulance run. As I ran out the door I had left eggs boiling on the stove. I had made this same mistake before, start a pot of water to boil eggs and right after putting the eggs in the hot water answer a page for a medical. The last time this was done was during my days on the fire department back in high school. I was back in 45 minutes and the last of the water has just boiled out of the pan.

In Montana ambulance runs tend to last over 4 hours since the nearest hospital was 90 miles away in Miles City. I got back to the bunkhouse with the smoke detectors ringing, smoke filled the house. The eggs had exploded when the water boiled away, except for the one egg that the shell had cracked during boiling, it was now a clump of blacken ash in the pan. The pan was ruined and I had opened all the windows and doors to clear the bunkhouse of the foul smoke that filled it. As the smoke cleared the smoke detectors stopped chirping and I settled into bed.

I had left the windows open all night to clear the smell of the brunt eggs and reported to Tim and Nate what had happened. The car was now packed and at Noon I started the long drive back to Minneapolis. First I stopped at the back to return the ambulance radio to Rex. I was going to miss Jordan and the friends I had made there.

Upper picture is of the T-rex casting in the Jordan Office of Charles M. Russell National Wildlife Refuge. Bottom picture for the 1st Brigade Combat Team of the Minnesota Army National Guard before leaving Camp Shelby, Mississippi for Operation Iraqi Freedom.

These two pictures were taken during my tour to Iraq. The upper was taken at LSA Anaconda, aka. Joint Base Balad as my group prepared to leave for Convoy Support Center Scania.

The bottom was taking during pass to Qatar with the skyline of Doha in the back group we enjoyed a tour of the bay.

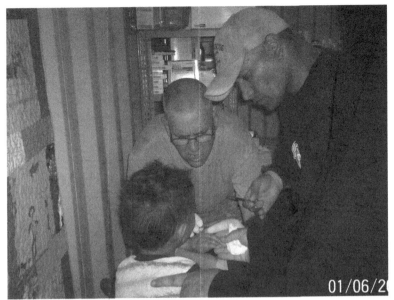

01/06/2(

Upper picture I was helping a fire fighter on his last day in Theater helping in our medical sections burn clinic that was outside of one of the gates at our camp. The clinic was built in a shipping container that was un-insulated. The heat of the day could be felt through the steel walls, however the burn victims would scream in pain if the air conditioner was turned on. For the patient we endured the warmth as best we could.

Bottom picture was finishing one of the many runs that were held at our camp.

HONEY I AM GOING TO IRAQ

I got home early Friday morning and had a couple hours of sleep before Jen dropped Kendra off. Kim had been babysitting for Jen over the summer and I was able to get up and answer the door when Jen arrived. Kendra almost leaped out of Jens arms when I opened the door and she wouldn't let go of me. We both fell asleep on the couch and woke up when Kim finally got up.

The attachment between Kendra and I reminded me of a long lost time when my own daughters were the same way. It was very refreshing to see that I can be a positive influence to so many of our friend's kids. I just longed for the day my daughters and I could reconnect.

Saturday morning I reported to guard drill, however I was to report to the office where I was handed my records and orders sending me to Iraq with the same unit I went to Korea with. My report date wasn't until November 12th. I would have over a month without work and with money we saved over summer we would still be short once I arrived Camp Shelby. We enjoyed the time we had together.

Kim screamed when I called her telling the news.

I had returned to the private adoption agency in hopes to

create some pathway to reconnect with the girls and see if there could be anything they could be a help with. Turned out I was to pay $200.00 per year per girl to have any services with the agency, when I pushed the issue of the deployment they reduced the fee to $200.00 a year, after the first year and still no responsible actions of support.

I refuse to pay any more money to the agency I had lost full trust and confidence in the agency with the past negative experience that I had experienced with their workers and condemnation of fatherhood. I was actually appalled at their fund raising campaign that they would start over the Christmas season. I feel that any money I was paying them was an extortion of their agencies past misrepresentation of birth fathers.

Their commercials are way too misleading and the constant hostile behavior to me remained as an unprofessional barrier that benefits no one and too ugly to participate in.

Still my focus was on getting through the deployment. It is just going through any deployment is hard enough, but the harshness of never being able to directly communicate with my children was torturous and inhumane.

Still to believe that this action is a form of social justice is misleading and misguided. Something better has to be done than all the indifference.

November came quickly

We departed as a group of late mobilization heading for our units that already spent the better half of a month at Camp Shelby. As we prepared to leave the Northeast Minneapolis Armory Kendra started to take her first real steps and began to walk all over the place. Final hugs to family and friends and on the bus the groups of soldiers got on for the plane that was waiting at the airport.

Hurricane Katrina had damaged much of the area, still the rifle ranges where in a horrible state of repair without the hurricane. Many of the pop-up targets had their centers shot out of them and could no longer detect a bullets passing through it. The maintenance staff there where simply lazy.

Transportation staff wasn't any better.

During a month long training activity at Fort Polk, Louisiana I was part of the Camp Shelby administrative staff that manages a large group of individuals who were either injured during training or had medical issues that interfered with their ability to complete the mission.

One afternoon eight soldiers were in downtown Hattiesburg for a mental health appointment when the Camp Shelby driver abandoned them at the clinic with no arrangement to assure pickup. We couldn't get them back to camp until 10pm. First there was the means to find the truck and the address of the clinic they were locked outside of.

Still overall it was a very successful month and soon everyone was back and getting ready for the flight over there.

We would spend Easter in Kuwait as we waited for our flight into Iraq. There was a brief stay at LSA Anaconda aka Joint Base Balad before getting onto CH47 Chinook cargo helicopters and the final ride to CSC Scania.

Once settled in I became the overnight base defense medic and Battalion Safety NCO. Though I was in a platoon sergeants position at first the unit was convinced to drop the platoon sergeants, by none other than the junior NCO from the old line unit just a few years ago. By the end of leave I found out what he had been doing in order to advance up his career progression. He had been undermining anyone who he did not want to follow and attempted to derail their careers in hope he could be promoted in their place.

One thing he did that helped my cause was during my leave another Staff Sergeant who was promotable to Sergeant First Class was sent to our unit to help out. Our problem NCO did to this new sergeant what he had done to others, worked with the leadership to denounce and have conflicting sergeant transfer out to another unit.

I was being kept on as a "patch" for all the training issues we didn't train for back at Camp Shelby. I got along with our lieutenant very well and the troubles our wonder boy caused a headache for everyone, but we all could endure through the deployment.

Memorial Day 2006 became a very traumatic day. Up to this day we were allowed to forward any Iraqi citizen with life, limb or eyesight health threats to the US Military Hospital in Baghdad. This morning started off very rough. Five critically burned citizens were delivered to a treatment clinic that was set up by a pervious group of medic's and was supported entirely with donated medical supplies from the United States.

Most of the victims were children between 2 and 12 years old burned at an accident at their home. A truck driver delivering fuel to burn bricks accidently ignites the fuel vapors with a cigarette light. He was trying to see how much fuel and oil was left in the tank as it gravity drained. The ensuing explosion was heard in our camp over 5 miles away and over 12 people were killed instantly at the scene with the remains of the driver never being found. Just before the badly burned surviving children of that tragic accident was one adult female in a household accident with a stove was brought to the clinic causing the activity of the day.

How our camp medical services was staffed was the unit I was a part of provided base defense coverage, medical support for area patrols and logistic support convoys. A separate medical unit provided troop medical clinic services. Our unit medics would assist the clinic during serious incidents that overwhelmed them like this day's incident.

It was basically a small clinic with a dental office, no lab or x-ray abilities any advance care required medical evacuation.

The MEDEVAC helicopter that was originally called was cancelled by the military hospital in Baghdad, the new group of medical staff would not honor anything beyond the basic army policy of no civilians unless they were injuries were caused by the collation forces.

Part was the fear the families were removing loved ones

from the meager Iraqi Hospital system in hopes that the Americans would have pitting on their conditions and let them receive better care or be able to send loved ones to the US for treatment.

Truth was for these two families the injuries the injuries were so severe that the Iraqi Hospital System was unable to care for and had released the victims to die peacefully at home. One child required assistance to breathe through and surgical airway we had to create. The little boy wouldn't make it back to the nearest Iraq Hospital. He passed away en route in the Iraqi ambulance which was an ambulance that only had a cot with no supplies on the shelves.

The rest of the burned victims would all die within the days following. It turned into a very long day. The burn victims arrived around 9 am and the last was evacuated to either the nearest Iraqi hospital or back to the family after 3 pm. I was going to read a bible passage for Memorial Service but as we finished up with the task of caring for the burn victims and the required reports that were filed I heard the bugle sound "Taps". I had missed the chapel services.

Both in Kosovo and Iraq child abuse and domestic violence was a part of their cultures and lifestyle. Both counties we saw the wounds of abuse. Both legs with suspicious burns, as if the child was dipped in boiling water or worst. Some had other wounds in various stages healing. Many of the wounds seen were right out of the text book. Yet no child protection services were available in either country.

Still we had a huge success. Of the living conditions that these children went home to and the complexity of their wounds none of the children developed infections and the wounds healed. We saw improvements each time they came to be seen in our clinic.

With the donations of medical supplies we had many stuff animal and children's toys to give away as well. We got to know many families well, but if we suspected child abuse all we could do was stay silent and non-judgmental and treat the wounds with no social services to report to.

Months later the lieutenant and I had found an article in a medical periodical explaining about a thing called Work Place Munchausen; this is where a coworker meets their emotional needs by creating unsolvable problems for their own self glorification. They get noticed as a problem solver since it is the problems they are creating that they able to solve. Actual issues and work place needs are forgotten and neglected.

This article mentioned about the hostile work environments that are created by such individuals. LT and I looked at each other and it made sense, stuck in Iraq wasn't going to solve the current problems with the problem NCO and the fact he was well connected didn't help.

Then the whole BCT got extended as part of the 2007 troop surge. My wife told me the news while I talked to her on the phone. By the time the deployment was over we would have over 22 months on federal active duty. I would not see home until late July 2007.

Our little truck stop was a small base to run one lap around the Living Area would be only 40 feet shy of a mile. For exercise I walked laps. If you wanted a longer walk there was the truck staging yard added an additional mile to the hike. As the safety NCO I had the advantage of getting the longer walk on a daily basis.

The advantage of a small base was whenever the insurgents would launch a rocket or mortar attack the first round was often shot over the camp, giving enough time for everyone to crawl into the nearest bunker before any additional rounds came in.

Of our time there we took over 200 incoming rounds fired at our camp in over 30 different attacks only few actually made it into the camp. Of those few rounds in the camp the most common injury was caused when people hit their heads entering their bunker. People actually got Purple Hearts for those injuries.

Three other events shaped this trip to Iraq; the first one

occurred November 16th when a civilian security company had stopped by to refuel and had supper. I was doing an evening walk as part of my physical training plan when I saw this civilian walking into the camp wearing ball cap he the initials "EMT" on it.

His name was Paul, a former Minnesota Police Officer who had moved to a western suburb of Minneapolis and took the job in Iraq as a way to pay off the house for his family. We talked for almost two hours. I had mentioned about my daughters, their adopted father was also on the same police department that he was once on.

He filled me in on what he witnessed as my daughters grew and were raised by their adopted family and wished me luck with their reunion. I had mentioned to him about the work I had been doing in the area of forest fire fighting and the contract opportunities that existed.

We talked about exchanging information and talking again when his convoy came back north.

Unfortunately the tragedy stuck, Paul was kidnapped that night when his detail arrived to meet their assigned convoy. It was an ambush, Paul and three other from the company were abducted. Only one video release from the captures was ever posted.

Their remains would not be discovered until almost 16 months later. He was such a gentle person and it was sad to see what the outcome of his tour really was. All around us there was contract group after contract group. At times the number of contractor to military personnel was 2 to 1 many unarmed and vulnerable.

The second incident occurred in December when a mortar attack hit the base. A third country national (TCN) had just stepped out of his truck to receive his supper when the round struck. He had a massive head wound and still breathing when we arrived with the ambulance.

MEDEVAC off the camp and to the military emergency

room. We found out he lived for an addition 10 hours past his wounding before passing away never regain consciousness.

The third incident was a massive attack that happened months later. Often the insurgents would fire some rocket to get everyone into the bunkers then waiting for the "All Clear" to be announced over the camp public address system before launching an aimed attack to the camp.

1:30am on a chili February morning I was leaving a toilet trailer in the housing area when the first round flew overhead. While on the night shift I would often walk around outside and do safety checks to the night work areas. I would announce on the camp radio whenever I heard a rocket or mortar pass overhead often offering those who had radios a few extra seconds to the bunkers before the second round or even the base PA system announced the attack. This night was no different from any of the other attacks we had endured.

Seeking shelter in the nearest bunker I was alone waiting for the numerous impacts to stop and for the "All Clear" that would put me to work with accountability and any other task this attack could cause. I dreaded the PA announcement it could be heard outside of the camp and it made you wonder who was listening.

Once the all clear was announced I went straight to my post attack position, it wasn't far, just less than 200 feet. One of our medics had started the three ambulances; we all had a gut feeling that sprang true in a very brief moment. The whistle of a mortar round came over head we scrambled into another nearby bunker as the explosion lifted me off my feet and threw me toward the bunker.

As I entered I was pelted with a small amount of gravel to my back. A call for casualties was announced over the radio and as the next round hit I was now moving toward the ambulance and heading out to get to the wounded.

In front of me rounds landed sending sparks in the air. I was far enough back and the ambulance had armor plating to the cab and armor windows, plus I had my body armor on as well, my concern was to the patients. I prayed that the insurgents would not back dial the tube and send more rounds back into the camp and on top of the wounded.

What we didn't know was at the same time a squad of soldier had drove into an ambush as well and both in the camp and in the patrol area we had casualties. MEDEVAC helicopters were now inbound and we moved the victims to the helipad stopping briefly at the Troop Medical Clinic to give doctors a chance to take care any additional needs before the flights.

Some of the soldiers were trained as Combat Life Savers and they did their jobs perfectly no need to delay for any additional care we took the injured to the waiting helicopters and all the injured were gone in less than fifteen minutes.

A kitchen staff member of Indian descent was killed in the attack and his remain was recovered. The camp was now dark as all the lights were turned off and our body armor would be worn until morning, just in case another attack was planned. The sight of flares being launched by the last MEDEVAC helicopter was an ominous sight, but then the camp became silent and dark.

Damaged buildings were everywhere in the camp, even the new chapel that our group was building had its roof damaged by shrapnel. The back wall of the MWR building was peppered through with the metal shards of the mortar rounds.

With the extension we all were offered a pass to Qatar. April was my turn to go, expecting some time to rest one of our guys in our group had a tragic accident involving a pocket knife. So on pass I geared up for work. Three hearings would be conducted over the incident and it was a hard lesion for the unit to learn.

Their company was made up of individuals that were recalled from the Inactive Ready Reserve. In order to prevent disagreements the company leadership loosens the basic rules and that when the problems started. An earlier late night ambulance run found one of their junior NCO's drunk, had fallen and had cut his head.

Another incident had a star cluster grenade detonate in the PX trailer we were using while a new building was being built, then after the accident in Qatar a bunker that was set up as a personal smoking lounge was set a fire.

By July I was more than ready to come home. It would be too late to join federal forest fire season and a month's leave was waiting. At Fort McCoy I volunteered for Courtesy Patrol for one last unit morale event and soon we leave for New Ulm, Minnesota.

First there was the Patriot Patrol that escorted us from Fort McCoy to New Ulm. Along the way more motor cycles joined the motorcade and at the Wisconsin, Minnesota border a Minnesota Highway Patrol car would take the lead.

Once off Interstate 90 the motorcade was large and grew even larger when fire trucks from New Ulm and the surrounding communities joined in. We went through New Ulm at parade speed and the scene at the New Ulm Civic Center was too much. As soon as we were released I got in the car and went home. Kim, mom and a church friend name Lester met me in New Ulm. I wanted to drive since it had been over a year since the last time I drove my car.

Once home we had some problems to render with bills and the car and then it was a planned road trip to Denver and up to Montana before settling down with the trucking company I had worked for prior to Kosovo.

By December I had a new unit. This was a Sergeant First Class position and for the stripes I volunteered to go with the unit for my second trip to Iraq. Kim had set up counseling for us in preparations of my return and the readjustment. The idea was not to wait for a problem form but be a head of the issues that lead to problems.

For me it was the best idea she have ever came up with. We used the next nine months as recovery period. There were issues with readjustments. I had accidently entered the woman's bathroom at church. I had periods of confusion, a constant ringing in the ears and a near constant headache once I got back. Traumatic Brain injury was still in the learning phase for medical staff and the Veterans Administration. I had made appointments for a TBI screening at the VA as well as Post Traumatic Stress Disorder sessions.

By February the headaches were mostly gone, the ringing in the ears has shown to be permanent, but the issues with the multiple traumatic events of my life remain a constant problem. Part of it is I truly do miss my girls and all the stalling to prevent me from seeing my girls still has a dramatic effect on my emotions. I have spent much of my life responding to problems and creating beneficial solutions for the people who survived serious injury as well as the effect of being an emergency responder.

The Termination of Parental Rights that I suffered through over 20 years ago has been a serious emotional injury and so far the social services solution had been indifference rather than to learn and improve. Through that social indifference I was expected to accept the role of a **"Deadbeat and undeserving of being a parent for any child."**

KIM'S DOCTOR CALLED

Shortly after reading every one for my next deployment we are called into see her doctor. Kim had developed throat cancer. I could have stayed home from the second deployment and nobody would have faulted me. Kim and I reviewed everything closely and decided that it would be better for us financially if I went on the deployment.

By Thanksgiving the trucking industry was at an all time low loads were seriously down from previous years. Most nights the company barely filled two trailers for Janesville, Wisconsin. So many nights I didn't have work. One night driving back from Janesville I stopped at a truck stop in Mauston.

A small kitten worked his way into the store and every time the poor thing was kicked out he found another way in. Four times he entered while I was n the store, the clerk asked if the kitten was mine. I told her at the third time he had entered the store; that if he approached me one more time I guess that meant he adopted me. Sure enough I stood at the counter and watched as he worked his way into the store and ran directly for me. He bumped my leg then dived over a stack of boxes that were in the isle waiting for the product to sock the shelves.

The clerk was allergic to cats and her eyes were puffy

and watering when I took him from her and headed for my truck. Driving back to Minneapolis he curled up at my neck and purred the whole way back never once getting upset at the noise and vibration of the truck and trailer. I now had two cats at home, the date was November 14th almost a year since meeting Paul, The kitten shown the same gentleness of Paul and was very much a peace keeper with our other cat Rascal.

Christmas was coming and we had no money for presents.

Snow storms provided the opportunity to make some cash during this lean time. The first storm I found a car in the ditch and an elderly gentleman attempting to change his flat tire on the shoulder of 35W by the County Road H2 on ramp in the north bound line.

I spent much of the day helping both drivers getting their cars back on the road. The older man's spare tire was bad and needed replacing. I took him to a Tires Plus nearby so he could get a new tire. He was on his way to a funeral and wouldn't make it. He had waited over two hours for a tow truck that never showed up. He gave me some money for taking my time to help him and went on his way.

Near Christmas Kim and I was leaving our church when we found a van stuck in the ditch dangerously close to a very busy intersection. Since as an EMT I make it a habit to stop at accidents, especially if there is a higher risk of a secondary accident. I had mounted a yellow warning light in my back window to alert other drivers of the incident and in hopes that the other drivers would slow down and shift to the other lane.

At this accident I was really missing the girls and although I try it must had been showing. The driver had buried his front end drive minivan deep into the ditch and the back wheel was still on the pavement. He asked if I was with any of the local fire departments and I told him no and why. I apologized for giving more information than his question asked for and told him that I was really badly missing my girls and why.

He said that was ok and gave me enough money to get Christmas presents for my brother's kids. As he drove off I could had sworn he looked like that social worker whose' actions had made me feel so lonely over the holidays, but I wasn't sure. I was glad that Kim and I didn't have to worry about presents. I never had asked for any money when I help someone stuck on the side of the road, I always let the ones I helped offer.

Work had kept me driving just enough to pay the basic bills and food, but nothing more. It was like that all the way to Valentine's Day before the loads picked up a little. At that time I started making the run from Minneapolis to Des Moines. It was steady but the loads remained light.

Kim was going through test and exams and found the tumor was actually quite advance. It was in a location were surgery would had been very disabling. The type of tumor though took special notice, it was human papaloma virus. Chemo and radiation would treat the tumor without any need for the surgery. However delays with TriCare insurance and some confusion between the providers held the needed treatment until May.

I would be at Fort Sill for pre-mob training before she would be done with her treatments. Another problem was the massive weight loss she would have during treatment causing the doctors to over radiate her and giving her a very bad burn that burned the esophagus shut.

The gastric bypass prevented her from taking in the full amount of liquid nourishment that the tube feeding was providing. Much of the feed was passing through her body without even digesting and the indwelling tube through her stomach always leaked. Since much of her feeding where done at night she became incontinent. Our home became her private nursing home.

The home health nurse and I trained friends to do her care procedures while I was away. I had taken a craft cart that I bought from Mills Fleet and farm and set it up as a nursing cart for her. Soon we had more medical supplies that we had places to store.

Between what the hospital provided and what medical supplies I had collected throughout the years we had enough stock to deal with any problem she presented.

For Kim's medical needs we needed to rebuild a bathroom for her to use safely and our church came to our rescue. Todd and Jessie built a beautiful bathroom for us. Our biggest problem was trying to keep our young kitten Cuddles from chasing the mice that were living under the trailer.

Our older cat Rascal would only go after the mice if they appeared in the common areas; Cuddles actually went straight for the nest in between the floor and the layer of insulation that protected the house from the Minnesota cold. He was earning his keep and showed a stubborn streak of going after what he wanted no matter what.

Still if either cat got outside they never got far, they hid under the house and waited to be called.

Mobilization date came up quickly; a last minute issue between the friends that would be helping us was dealt with and we were sure I was still able to go on deployment. I had explored the possibility of delaying my departure until the problems were fully addressed and I was sure the plan would work without causing any need to come home early.

Back at Fort Sill the units were crammed into billets that were designed to hold half the troops that were in there now. Air conditioner units could not keep up with the body heat, each night was miserable. Adding to the problems were the many old ghosts of my time that I was active duty there.

First the billets we were assigned to where near a location of a body I helped recover, 26 year ago. The body had been decaying in the woods for 4 months and found by those two boys.

Second was the old hospital were the girls were born. It was now the Mob Station and the old morgue was the briefing room. The chair I sat in my neck hairs were raised I could feel the many trips I took to that very same spot 26 years prior: each story came back alive, as the briefer spoke; the old ghosts flew around me.

The old chapel where I met my first wife was now gone, changed into a store room. I could look down the hall and remember the week of the tornados and the pride of holding my daughters when they were born. For two and a half months sleep nearly escaped me. Getting on line I found both daughters Facebook pages.

I attempted to connect but never received any word back from them. My oldest immediately locked me out of her account, but the youngest remained open to view. She never replied to any of my communications. Eventually both would shut down their Facebook accounts.

I was able to get some up to date pictures of them.

Still all this made my longing for them even more.

I had typed out my history of the dealing with county social services and sent it to the Democratic presidential candidates. One candidate would answer **"What does this have to do with me?"** another kept communications going on even after the election.

By August the training was done. For many much of the training was already done before even arriving to Fort Sill, I was continually told to just take it easy however once in country there would be a lot of work to keep me busy.

Beginning of August everyone had a chance to take leave or if we stayed locally a pass. With the multiple deployments bonuses were now being earned through extra leave time. I took the leave to make sure Kim was doing as ok as she tried to make the telephone calls sound. Besides if I calculated it properly I could be spending much of the following summer on leave rather than being able to be on fire crew again.

Once home I found a problem. In reviewing Kim's medicine with her nurse we found two medications that were clashing and causing Kim to be horribly confused. A call to the doctor and medications were readjusted. She was out of the confusion as soon as the one medication worn off within a couple of days.

By now Kim had a team of doctors and it was going to be work just to keep the information straight.

That leave went by too quickly. We did get to spend some time with Jimmy. He was thinking about setting up a dog training business and had a beautiful Siberian husky he picked up in China. He found out very quickly my love for dogs and dog handling. We talked about both of our business ideas and how both could help each other. Jimmy returned to China to continue his work there shortly after I got back to the deployment.

Kim was getting better and stronger each day now that the conflicting pill worked its way out of her system. With the chemo and radiation done she was completely cancer free and soon she would start the procedures to reopen her esophagus.

Nothing was working. Because of her medical needs I was one of the first people in the unit to go home on leave once leave cycles started. Meanwhile the work I was warned about was starting. I was prepared to take on the tasks of battalion fire safety representative and unit prevention leader (which means I collect the monthly urine samples for drug abuse prevention).

What we were not expecting was what we found once we got to Joint Base Balad. I was not prepared for a counterpart on my arrival. So when I was told I didn't have a counterpart to guide me it was without surprise. Once at the clinic I took my directions from both the medical platoon leader and my medical operations officer.

First day I walked both sides of the camp finding every possible resource we may need to do our clinics job. The main focus was the fact we provided emergency medical coverage to the west side of camp which was itself a small village of over 12,000 occupants, many where civilian contract employees that may or may not have their own organic medical support.

Our predecessors just dealt with each call as it came without any risk assessments or emergency preplanning, they never worried about being ready for the emergency. We had stepped in behind an eight ball.

Of the three ambulances assigned to the clinic none were clean each covered with over a half an inch of dust both inside and out. Iraq was such dirty place and the previous unit wouldn't spend each day keeping the ambulances clean. Only one ambulance was set up for emergency response all of the ambulances were in different stages of disrepair with one needing a complete rebuild.

Matter of fact the whole clinic area was covered with exposed medical supplies. Three container units were recovered from the miss-ship lot by the group and they never inventoried what the stashed and left exposed to the sun and dirt.

Our group went to work cleaning the place up and discovering that many of the supplies stashed around the clinic were either damaged by the weather and heat or had already expired.

Within a few days a suicide by our Post Exchange shown another problem that was handed to us none of the emergency services agencies were talking to each other. Listening to the radio communications I turned to our admin major and simply said "I have a lot of work to do.'

I spent the week setting up a meeting with the fire department, other ambulance services and the military police. Once the meetings started the fire chief took control and the most successful meetings of the deployment begun. We got more handheld radios for the clinic and for the ambulances as well as the medical administration vehicle.

It took nearly three weeks of research to develop the emergency medical services response plan for our ambulances. Not able to find anything else in writing to back up and support the tasking of providing the emergency medical services we had been asked to do. I documented a plan to hopefully keep our medics safe and the emergency response effective then presented to the medical leadership.

So to work I went.

A month into the job and my leave period came up. Before Kim was diagnosis with the tumor we thought about maybe meeting in Germany and have the leave there. Now that changed. I got home in time for the first procedure to reopen Kim's esophagus failed. It was around Thanksgiving that I took leave and we had some time with both mine and Kim's family before the second surgery failed to open her throat.

It wouldn't be until I returned to Iraq before a procedure succeeded to get through the scar tissue and begin the process to stretch her esophagus to its normal size and hopefully Kim could start eating again. However doctors could never successfully reopen her throat. Another surgery would have to be planned. In order for her to live and be able to eat again, she would have to lose her ability to speak.

My daughters adopted mother sent out a seasonal e-mail to the family and this time I was included. I am very thankful for the e-mail and for being on Thanksgiving Day it gave me both hope and something to pray for, **May this be the last year I remain separated from my daughters**.

The holidays have been always difficult. Never being able to have the girls over for thanksgiving or to share Christmas presents leave a hallow feeling whenever I go to my brother or sisters house for gatherings. I haven't placed a star on the Christmas tree since that first Christmas divided. Never know if I will ever have a star on my tree; that was the kids' task each Christmas.

However an e-mail from my oldest daughter around Christmas called me **"Untrustworthy and unreliable for failing to simply stay quiet and out of their lives."** They are not ready to take me back into their life and all the attempts that I make are viewed as a selfish scheme only for me and not what they want from me. They want me to silently forget they exist.

That when I went to Combat Stress and look for some help that was directed for us fathers. What I found were some changes. However has thing completely changed yet?

A compounding problem for me is how do I stay silent for another 20 years and never be able to let them know I care. Somewhere somehow I need to be able to try. The never ending dilemma and proof that the social worker was good with his words **"Everything will be done to prevent your daughters from ever wanting you're in the rest of their lives."**

The best news was that for once I wasn't accused of hiding something. I found an ear to talk to. Not just someone recognizes that the policies of many of our nations' child protection agencies are failing, but a social service expert who has seen the failure of the child protection service. Mainly because of the things I discussed she saw in her own office back home in the U.S.

She was blessed to have an attorney in her area that didn't pass the fathers along to suffer. She had caught and fired social workers using the tactics that were used in the case that removed my rights. She as well recognized that many families were failed by the child protection policies of the 1980s and 90s and many children have been harmed by the harsh ideology, worst yet knowing that such blind ideology often prevents children in dangerous families from gaining the needed services.

HARD BUS RIDE HOME.

May 17th 2009 my group of soldiers loaded up in a choice of three buses to take us back home to Minnesota. Our deployment over and it was time to return to our families. I knew my wife and mom would be there. Two of my brothers and one of my nephews would be there as well. I kept everyone informed of my of m progress as we headed west to St. Paul.

But the pain of knowing that my daughters would never be there and the heart ache of confirming their absence only showed that for life my ex-wife's anger will remained rewarded. Still too there are many people that I know who claim they believe as a father I have earned and deserve this cold treatment and that I am selfish for wanting a positive caring relationship with my girls.

To make home knowing again I could not legally write to my daughters, call my daughters, send their gifts to them. I am to be believed to be so bad I am undeserving for any connection or contact with them?

Could any parent tolerate constantly being told that you're forbidden to have any right, role or act of love for your children? How could this mentality be the proper ideology for the good of any family?

I plan no harm for anyone, just to let those who work in the social services field to look beyond petty ideologies and consider all feelings. Look for the truth don't think that because you bare in a position of power you are entitled to seek revenge for someone else or a scapegoat to take the place of someone who did you wrong or through misunderstanding seek to harm.

Too much harm has already been done. The course of action desired by someone whose dad was a drunk, abusive, or abandon them didn't make me a dad who was the same or deserving to the harsh actions. To judge that my love for my daughters as selfish act on my part is a blind and selfish thought in its own right. To deny any parent their rights to their child without first convicting them lawfully for abuse, neglect or abandonment is an obstruction of justice and an act of social violence as well as an act of kidnapping.

Involuntary Termination of Parental Rights for the need of someone desire of revenge or anger is not what the law was designed for. To scheme for such a harsh and violent act is a criminal act that is embraced by too many county child protection services, as well as the media.

It is a short cut not requiring full investigations or proper case management which includes full and truthful documentation. Too many cases like my family have tied up the system and wasted easily billions of hard earned taxpayer dollars while endangered children where left in the hands of a known dangerous parent.

Multiple parenting evaluations, actual and direct case management and a factual investigation must be a part of each child protection case. Referrals for services must be done by the social worker, they know where the services are and it is a disservice to make any parent to search for services that the worker and simply pick up the telephone and make the initial appointment. Any unprofessional action by social workers should be should be investigate for conspiracy to kidnap and the worker removed from the profession not just the case.

Too many times a polarized social services case is the fault of both the social worker and the parents involved. It is the obligation of the county social services for the good of the child to reassigning social workers when a case becomes polarized and not up to the parent to stomach through the violate behavior of the county services. Only after a change in social worker can any county social service even consider the process of termination of parental rights and even then it should only be reserved when an actual conviction of abuse, neglect or abandonment occurs first.

Sadly any involuntary termination of parental rights for any other cause, than as part of the process beyond criminal conviction is only an act of control and abuse in its own right and an act of kidnapping and must be treated as a criminal intend not to falsely believe that it is in a social best interest..

The states, not the counties should have the authority to remove parental rights. Too often within the county social services and courts develop a relationship that actually caused TPR without the judge fully reviewing the case, only to look for what the judge wanted to hear in order to simply sign the order away. By removing this relationship at the county level then the county will have to ensure all appropriate services and action where done first and not just simply claim such without validation of such services.

I love my kids and all I want is to just one day to spend time or a meal with them.

IT CAME IN A DREAM

Within months after the death of my dad I had a very vivid dream. I have often marveled at the simple ways God attempts to talk to us. Too often we are so self absorbed that we can never hear God talking to us. But the dream remains as the great proof to Gods existence for me. For me it was truly a vision.

I knew at age 13 that I would be in the military and the fire fighting and the successes and failures of my life. The pain of many years of separation before a reunion would be enjoyed. I seen the forest fires that I had fought as well as the entry into some of the house fires I had found responding too. Still I never consider myself as anything other than a person with a vivid dream.

I had a rough idea of the girls I would date and who would become my wife. Maybe I was scared at the dream as I witnessed things happening in my life. Maybe I was fighting to prevent the heart I knew was coming. Maybe it was the pain of over three years of being told, if she was mad enough I was too loose everything.

Still the dream was a simple means of using the knowledge of the time to speak of a life to come. Now I look back at that life and see the path God blazed through me. Of all the places that were better after my squad or unit had left and the changes that stayed in place.

I noticed it at once at Fort Sill when the military police responded with the hospital ambulance to an accident as we reported in for the deployment. Something I did as an E-4 Specialist remained in action 24 years later, now as a policy not just the habit of a street wise responder who wouldn't approach a scene without police support.

In Kosovo the training with the Kamenica Fire Department and the relationship that developed between the community and the American forces. I pray that we helped developed a lasting peace in that land and for a renewed prosperity for the countries that were part of the former Yugoslavia.

Pray that through God's blessing this rough path I have been sent on can provide a smoother lane of travel for those whom follow. And for my daughters a path home to a father who loves and waits for them.

In the meantime I remain a simple mustard seed and pray to service my nation, community, church and family.

WRITING A FINAL CHAPTER

There are many people that through their action helped me write this book. I know reading this book some would be angry at how my words represents their actions and the effects to my life. I pray that together we can write a better final chapter.

I have many hopes and may the blessing of the book help created a greater blessing for all. I look forward to writing a positive ending to this book someday.

As for the reader this story is true and it is the side of the story that was demanded to stay silent for others wanted to believe what they wanted the truth to be. That is why there was no full investigation, no criminal charges ever filed, no jury of peers. I was never allowed to make a statement, never allowed for those witnesses who could validate my words a chance to speak.

Worst yet the selfish actions of a court appointed attorney and the lack of will by the remaining lawyers I contacted for support the right of appeal was obstructed. Such actions do not meet anyone's best interest.

As for my daughters, I know you have been raised well, I do not intend to harm or deny that relationship. However anyone that demands any relationship to be denied needs to be considered suspect of their true intentions, which sadly is mostly a desire to harm for personal cause.

All I pray for a dinner day, a holiday gathering and occasional telephone calls, letters and e-mails. As for my youngest daughter I offer my support for joining the Air Force as well as both girls college graduation, for I am proud of both of you.

I pray for that living day we can meet each other and be some form of a family again with a positive and nurturing relationship. I pray this in all of our best interest.

My heart and door remains open for my children. I look forward to the day we all reach out to each other in faith, love and the blessing of God.

I am thank that I have tried to tell my story for over 20 years and for all those who pushed me away and told me to; **"Buck it up, get over it or you deserve it so take it like a man."** Now nearly 25 years later I was being asked for the first time to tell my full story, to continue to tell the whole story. Still there were those who still didn't want to hear any part of the story. In difference was still mostly due by victims other crimes of child abuse, domestic violence, sexual assault or harassment not willing to accept that the same sex that had attacked them could also be a victim.

Still someone wants to listen, that is a great step forward, now to get the right people to hear so that no one would ever have to endure needless and painful family separations.

THINGS I LEARNED ALONG THE WAY

First lesson learned is that the greatest act of unfaithfulness isn't infidelity; but rather to scheme and conspire against each other. To plan out how you want to hurt the person whom for better or worse to live out your lives together. Just to prove how angry you are at them is a dangerous act of unfaithfulness.

Second lesson is that discrimination knows no color, culture, religion or sex for discrimination is a blindness created by the darkness deep in our own heart. Discrimination is fueled by hate and misunderstanding and doesn't change until we open our hearts to each other.

Third lesson is to love unconventionally and forgive completely. For the reader you may feel this book is reflected by my anger of what we all went through. However the truth is I just want to have the means to use this story to help social workers become better at their jobs and protect the needy families from the vulnerability of inappropriate attitudes.

Another lesson learned is how some can be chosen to live the Bible not just simply read it. That often when someone is enduring a grand test we rarely see it until after the person either dies or someone achieve an unexplainable success. God has many ways to talk to us and ask us to help the almighty in a special tasking. I guess this is how God trains his angles.

The final lesson is the grace and mercy of God. We rarely cheer someone through the hard times and the testing our lord puts us through. Too often we are only so self absorbed that the message is missed and the blessing forgotten. Through those periods where I could have been looking at the face of our Lord, I have only learned to value life even more.

This book was written as a form of therapy, written by request of a mental health worker who had witnessed some of the same abuses that I had endured and was willing to talk about. My prayer is that more suffering parents be able to find the ability to speak out and change our world again. Like a young lady did nearly 50 years ago.

Printed in the United States
by Baker & Taylor Publisher Services